BLACK+DECKER™

THE BOOK OF
HOME
HOW-TO

COMPLETE PHOTO GUIDE TO
HOME REPAIR

Wiring • Plumbing • Floors • Walls • Windows & Doors

The Editors of Cool Springs Press

COOL
SPRINGS
PRESS

Brimming with creative inspiration, how-to projects, and useful information to enrich your everyday life, Quarto Knows is a favorite destination for those pursuing their interests and passions. Visit our site and dig deeper with our books into your area of interest: Quarto Creates, Quarto Cooks, Quarto Homes, Quarto Lives, Quarto Drives, Quarto Explores, Quarto Gifts, or Quarto Kids.

23 22 21 20 19   2 3 4 5

ISBN: 978-0-7603-6625-7

Digital edition published in 2019
978-0-7603-6626-4

The content in this book appeared in the previously published titles from Cool Springs Press:
BLACK+DECKER Carpentry Made Simple
BLACK+DECKER The Book of Home Improvement
BLACK+DECKER The Complete Guide to Bathrooms, 5th Edition
BLACK+DECKER The Complete Guide to Plumbing, 7th Edition
BLACK+DECKER The Complete Guide to Wiring, 7th Edition
BLACK+DECKER The Complete Photo Guide to Home Repair, 4th Edition
BLACK+DECKER Wood Floors

Library of Congress Cataloging-in-Publication Data available.

Design & Page Layout: *tabula rasa* graphic design
Photography: Photography by Rich Fleischman (with assistance from Charles Mossey, Erik Sateren, and Tom Tschida), except pages 28, 43, 46, and 104 via Shutterstock

BLACK+DECKER The Book of Home How-To Complete Photo Guide to Home Repair

Created by: The Editors of Cool Springs Press, in cooperation with BLACK+DECKER.

BLACK+DECKER and the BLACK+DECKER logo are trademarks of The Black & Decker Corporation and are used under license. All rights reserved.

Printed in China

NOTICE TO READERS

CONTENTS

For even the most seasoned home repair expert, gaining experience begins with one project. It might be as simple as painting a wall or unclogging a sink. Then, he or she might tackle a drafty window and then a damaged floorboard. As the projects mount, confidence grows and comfort level increases. Soon, the budding DIYer attains a new level of self-sufficiency. Then, when a new problem or challenge arises, it can be dealt with immediately and at little or no cost. That is the goal.

The home repair projects featured in this book were chosen because they are the ones a new home-owner is most likely to encounter: and they are achievable even for folks with little or no DIY experience and only a handful of basic tools. They range in difficulty from the quick and simple to the somewhat more ambitious and time consuming. But each featured project or skill is shown in full detail with clear color photos and comprehensive, step-by-step instructions.

Sure, these days you can go online and find dozens or hundreds or thousands of articles and videos that claim to show you how to fix your house.

Some are helpful, others are incomplete or even wrong. In *BLACK+DECKER The Book of Home How-To Complete Photo Guide to Home Repair* you can be assured and confident that the information and guidance you find is reliable and exceptionally helpful. We have been making books like this for more than 30 years using a vast network of professional tradespeople to guide the information. But perhaps the best reason to own this book and keep it close at hand is that you will always know where to find the information—no backtracking over dozens of links or discovering that the information you were using is missing or has changed.

So consider this book to be something of a primer for your new adventure in home ownership and home care. You can find many other home repair books that are far thicker than this one and tackle many more projects, including several in the BLACK+DECKER family. But we are confident that the carefully chosen projects featured here will help you solve the home repair projects that are the most likely to come up. Thank you for relying on us to get you started in your handy career and best of luck!

Floorcoverings wear out faster than other interior surfaces because they get more traffic. And so they require more maintenance. The issue with floors is not just cosmetic: surface damage can affect more than appearance. Scratches or gouges in resilient flooring and cracks in grouted tile joints let moisture into the floor underlayment, leading to rot. Whether your floorcovering is wood strips, parquet, sheet vinyl, laminate, or anything else, it is helpful to view it as a protective membrane for the bones of your house.

Bathroom floors suffer the most from moisture problems, with kitchen floors coming in a close second. You can fix most problems yourself, including squeaks, scratches and dents, and other minor damage to floorcoverings.

There is a reason that some flooring products are described as "low maintenance." If you are considering installing new floorcoverings, maintenance is definitely something to think about. In very broad terms, on the next page is a ranking of floorcoverings and their maintenance requirements. It is also worth knowing this information if you are interested in keeping your current floorcoverings in good repair: some types simply require more attention than others.

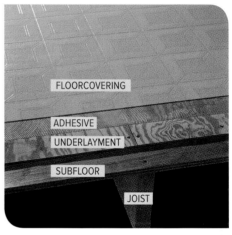

In a typical residence, the floors in the habitable spaces have a foundation of subfloor (usually ¾" plywood or oriented strand board) attached to the floor joists. The subfloor is too rough and uneven to serve as a good substrate for floorcoverings, so it is usually covered with a thin (¼" thick is typical) underlayment of sanded plywood or lauan plywood. The floorcovering is bonded to the underlayment (sheet vinyl or nonceramic tile). Ceramic tile is bonded to an underlayment of cementboard, not plywood. Laminate "floating" floors rest on the underlayment without attachment—the individual flooring strips interlock and typically "float" on a thin, cushiony pad. Traditional hardwood strip flooring is nailed down, usually with an underlayment of rosin paper or, in older homes, tar paper.

FLOORING MAINTENANCE REQUIREMENTS BY TYPE

- **Wood Strip Flooring.** *Solid wood flooring is seldom installed in high-moisture areas, but in other parts of the house it is very common and is considered to be a strong selling point for a home. Most "gleaming" wood flooring is hardwood, primarily oak and maple. Softwood floors such as pine are beautiful but less durable and typically are reserved for low-impact areas, like dining rooms or bedrooms. Wood floors are among the biggest demanders when it comes to maintenance. Not only are they prone to surface damage, they are natural products and subject to dimensional stresses from changes in atmospheric humidity. They require periodic refinishing, which is a major project.*

- **Ceramic Tile.** *Tile floors are very popular for good reasons. They are resistant to moisture and relatively easy to clean, making them good choices for kitchens and baths. They are also easy for DIYers to install. And tile manufacturers pay close attention to design trends, so if you are remodeling, a ceramic tile floor can offer cutting-edge design features. Made of ceramic or porcelain, the tiles themselves are quite durable, although they will chip or break if you drop a cast iron pan. The main maintenance issue with tile is grout lines. Grout is a cementitious material, but contains additives so it can flex a bit as it fills the gaps between tiles. After a while grout loses its flexibility and starts to crumble. It also is susceptible as a host for mold and is prone to staining and discoloring.*

- **Sheet Vinyl.** *Low maintenance to the extreme. Current products have greatly expanded the traditional styles, which have suffered from plainness. Not a high-end floorcovering, but as long as you keep it in good repair it can function for many years with just some sweeping and mopping.*

- **Laminate Flooring.** *Laminate strip flooring has greatly expanded its market share in the past decades. It's cheap, looks more or less like wood, and is relatively easy to install. It is also formulated from relatively cheap materials, including what is basically a photograph of the flooring beneath a wear layer of aluminum oxide. It is difficult to patch up if you get a dent or scratch because there is not much material to work with.*

- **Carpeting.** *Wall-to-all carpeting is essentially in its own separate category when it comes to floorcoverings. But it is a common home material and one that definitely needs attention—often beyond the basics of vacuuming and occasional steam-cleaning. If you are having it installed, here's a good tip: obtain and save any leftover carpeting. It can be used for patching. You can also find usable carpeting in closets and other out-of-the-way spaces to claim for repairing carpet damage in the more visible living areas.*

CLEANING & MAINTAINING A WOOD FLOOR

Cleaning resilient floor surfaces like sheet vinyl and ceramic tile is pretty easy—basically, you sweep or vacuum and then mop. Wood floors, however, are a bit trickier. With wood floors it is important to evaluate the floor carefully before charging in with a bucket of soapy water. The type of finish and its condition are critical in choosing the right type of cleaning products and methods.

Wood floors are among the most durable flooring materials you can install, but like any flooring, they require occasional maintenance to preserve their look and function. Years of regular use can wear out the surface finishes, and even the hardest woods can be scratched by pets with sharp toenails or by furniture dragged along their surface. Impact by heavy items—tools or even heavy dishes—can dent a wood floor. And the biggest enemy of all is water.

Begin by sweeping, vacuuming, then removing dust from the floor using a pad-mop equipped with a wet pad. Scuff marks can be lightly scrubbed by hand using a soft cloth, not an abrasive pad.

How to Evaluate & Clean Wood Floors

If the floor finish is not sound, water will soak into the wood immediately. Do not clean with a water-based product, because it will stain and damage the floor. Instead, clean the floor with cloths dampened with mineral spirits. An unsound floor finish will eventually need to be either recoated with the same finish currently on the floor or rewaxed.

Next, test to see if your floors have a paste wax finish. Slightly dampen a piece of extra-fine steel wool and rub the floor in several areas. Paste wax will show up by leaving a gray smudge on the steel wool pad. On a paste-wax floor, clean the floor with cloths moistened with odorless mineral spirits. Let dry completely, then apply a new coating of paste wax, and buff it thoroughly, following manufacturer's directions.

NOTE: NEVER apply a finish coat over a waxed floor.

Does your floor have an acrylic wax? These newer waxes are best identified by the dirty, patch-like appearance they have as they begin to wear. If your floor has this kind of synthetic wax, use an ammonia-based wax stripper to remove the wax layer, then apply a new layer of acrylic wax. Be aware that acryllc waxes will need frequent reapplication.

REMOVING STAINS FROM WOOD FLOORS

Just about anything can stain wood floors. Many stains are surface discolorations that may be able to be removed with nothing more than a light scraping or rubbing with an abrasive pad or fine sandpaper. Always try this before reaching for more serious solutions, some of which require the use of dangerous chemicals.

Some stains, especially water stains or stains from pet urine, can soak very deeply into the wood and are difficult or impossible to fully remove. In these instances, you should consider replacing entire floorboards. Another solution is to use a bleach to lighten the color of the stain. Be aware, though, that bleach does not remove a stain, but just lightens it. After bleaching, you will likely be left with the task of restaining the bleached area to match the surrounding floor.

Products you may need to remove stains from a wood floor include extra-fine nylon scrubbing pad (A); sharp scraper (B); sandpaper (C); mineral spirits (D); lacquer thinner (E); oxalic acid (F); putty knife (G); chlorine bleach (H); protective gloves (J); eye protection (K); Goof Off stain remover (L); baking soda (M); and vinegar (N).

GUIDE TO DEALING WITH WOOD FLOOR STAINS

Paint. Obvious drips can often be scraped off with a sharp paint scraper. If the paint has penetrated into the wood you should be able to remove it with light sanding with a scrub pad or fine sandpaper. A commercial removal product, such as Goof Off, may also work well.

Crayon, black heel marks. Try a water-based cleaner first, then a cloth lightly dampened with mineral spirits.

Gum. Chill with ice and chip off; or try mineral spirits.

Fingernail polish. Moisten a cloth with lacquer thinner, and carefully dab the stain. Avoid getting it on the rest of the finish, as it will likely dissolve it. After removal, you may have to touch up the finish.

Glue. Most wood glues or household glues are water based. Begin by trying to simply scrape away the glue. Next, try a water-based cleaner. Last resort: a chemical removal product, like Goof Off.

Construction adhesive. Chip away as much as you can, then apply steam with a household iron, and try to scrape away as much as possible. Remaining adhesive may need to be sanded away.

Coffee and tea. Dilute ¼ cup of apple cider vinegar in 1 gallon of water and use a sponge to moisten the stain. Let it sit for 1 to 2 hours, then scrub with a clean sponge. Rinse with a damp sponge and dry immediately.

Water, iron rust stains. Mix a solution of oxalic acid and water, following label directions. Apply the solution carefully to the stain and wait several hours, or overnight. Thoroughly wash away the residue with water mixed with baking soda, which neutralizes the acid. Oxalic acid is caustic, so make sure to wear protective gloves and avoid getting it on your skin. This solution will lighten the wood, and you may need to sand and restain the area to match the surrounding floor.

Grape juice, dye, blood. Apply household bleach to the stain and blot it up. If it does not remove the stain immediately, reapply and let sit overnight. Neutralize the bleached area with vinegar, then rinse with clear water. If the bleach has removed too much wood color, restain the area to match surrounding wood.

Urine. Use a product like Klean Strip, which is a mixture of hydrogen peroxide and sodium hydroxide. This is very caustic and toxic material, so handle carefully. Apply the bleach and let stand as directed. Rinse with clear water. This product will bleach the wood quite light, so staining and refinishing the area will be necessary.

How to Use Wood Bleaches

Choose a bleach appropriate for the stain.
Wearing protective gloves, apply the bleach
solution to the stain area, being careful to confine
it to that area. Let the bleach remain on the stain
for the recommended time, then neutralize the
bleach with the recommended agent (baking
soda solution for oxalic acid, vinegar solution for
household bleach, clear water for Klean Strip).
Wash the area thoroughly with clear water, wipe
up excess water, and let dry.

Once dry, lightly sand the area. All bleaches will raise the wood grain, and before applying a wood stain, the grain must be sanded smooth.

Apply a rub-on wood stain that closely matches the tone of the surrounding floor using a soft rag. Let dry completely, then carefully apply a polyurethane or other matching surface finish to blend the stain area with the surrounding floor.

Most scratches and dents in solid wood floors can be repaired. Dents occur when wood fibers become compressed. If the wood fibers are not broken, dents can often be removed by expanding the wood fibers using heat and moisture. Whatever repair you attempt, confine your work as narrowly as possible to the damaged area only—the smaller the repair area, the less noticeable it will be.

Often the trickiest part in making a scratch or dent disappear is matching and blending the surrounding finish. This is especially true if you end up taking sandpaper to the damage area, so view sanding as a last resort. Most hardware stores and flooring specialty stores sell touch up pens or pencils in a range of tints. These are worth a try. If you don't find an exact match, choose one that is slightly darker rather than lighter.

If the easy fixes fail and the scratch is still there, then you'll need to go for the sandpaper and perhaps some wood putty. Here's how to do it.

How to Repair Shallow Scratches

Sweep the floor clean, then wash the area around the scratch with a cloth moistened with odorless mineral spirits. Let the floor dry. With fine or very fine sandpaper (150 grit), lightly sand the scratched area, sanding parallel to the wood grain and periodically wiping away the sanding dust. It is possible that light sanding will remove the scratch if the damage is only in the surface finish.

After the scratch is removed, clean the area with mineral spirits, let dry, and lightly touch up the surface with the same finish used on the rest of the floor, restoring its shine.

How to Repair Deep Scratches

Clean the scratched area with odorless mineral spirits, then lightly sand away the surface finish down to bare wood, using 150-grit sandpaper. For faster results use a random orbit sander. For more control, hand sand.

When the bare wood is exposed, carefully apply a nonwax wood filler to the crack. Colored wood fillers may be available that closely match the color of your floor. If not, you can apply an uncolored wood filler, then stain it to match the floor. After the filler dries, lightly sand it. Wipe away all dust, then apply a rub-on wood stain or finish with a small brush, if needed. Reapply as needed.

How to Repair Dents

Clean the area around the dent, then sand the dented area with fine (150-grit) sandpaper to completely remove the surface finish down to bare wood. Sand very lightly past the damage area to "feather it in" so you do not have any hard ridges of finish.

Moisten a clean cloth with water and place it over the dent. Apply the hot tip of a household clothes iron over the wet cloth, moving it around to drive moisture down into the wood fibers. Try to avoid steaming the surrounding wood finish, as it may discolor it. The dented area should soon swell back, eliminating the dent. Let the wood dry completely overnight. Sand the area lightly, if necessary, and remove the dust. Carefully apply finish touch-ups to match the rest of the floor.

Loose floorboards can be extremely obvious or as subtle as a faint squeak. Deciding whether to fix the problem should start by questioning if the loose board or boards present any kind of a tripping hazard. If so, naturally, the floorboards should be secured. This can be done either from above, working through the surface or edges of the floorboard, or from below if you have access to the joists to which the floorboards are fastened. Simple squeaks are another matter. If they irritate you, the remedies are generally easy to effect. Or you can choose to live with the squeak—it's a good way to keep tabs on your kids.

Solutions for Loose Floorboards

The surest way to reattach loose or buckled floorboards is driving new fasteners from above. Start by drilling pilot holes for several flooring nails in the floorboard only. The nail will grip better if you do not predrill the wood underlayment and subfloor. Flooring nails are spiral or ribbed for better gripping power.

Existing flooring nails may have simply loosened from the underlying subfloor, allowing the floor to buckle upward. Look for nail heads securing the flooring, and use a nail set to drive them back down into the subfloor. If the nails are hidden in the tongue-and-groove joints, drill pilot holes on the loose floorboards, and drive finish nails down into the subfloor. Recess the nail heads with a nail set, then fill the holes with wood putty.

Solutions for Squeaky Floors

Find the source of the squeak, if possible. Look for flexing or gaps between the subfloor and joists. Fill these areas with shims glued into place or with construction adhesive that will dry hard and eliminate the space for movement (right). This method also works if you spot areas where the subfloor is flexing and rubbing against pipes or HVAC ducts.

Install solid cross blocking between joists to reinforce the floor and eliminate the squeak by eliminating flexing. Apply a bead of construction adhesive along the top of the blocking, then nail it to the adjoining joists so it is flush up against the subfloor.

The squeaking may also be caused by gaps between the surface flooring and the subfloor. The solution here is to drive screws from below, drawing down the surface flooring and snugging it up against the subfloor

REPLACING DAMAGED FLOORBOARDS

There will be instances in which flooring boards are too badly damaged or stained to be repaired with acceptable results. In these instances, replacing the boards will be the best option, and in most cases it will be possible to do this in a way that makes the repair invisible to all but the keenest eye.

On a solid hardwood floor, a very good time to replace floorboards is when you are already planning on sanding and refinishing. Once the replaced flooring is installed, a complete

sanding down to bare wood will nicely blend in the original floor with the new replacement boards.

Whenever possible, hardwood boards should be replaced along their entire length, not just patched in as a short segment. A replacement board running full length and matching the pattern of the other boards will be almost invisible, especially if the entire floor is being refinished. Where this is not possible, you can outline the damaged area, cut it away with a circular saw and chisel, and cut a tight-fitting replacement piece to insert in the space.

Ideally, floorboards are replaced in full lengths so the original pattern can be preserved. However, it is sometimes most expedient to replace only the damaged area with small, custom-cut segments and do your best to blend it in.

How to Replace a Hardwood Plank

Use an oscillating multitool to cut the end of a hardwood plank. These relatively new power tools are good for making isolated cuts.

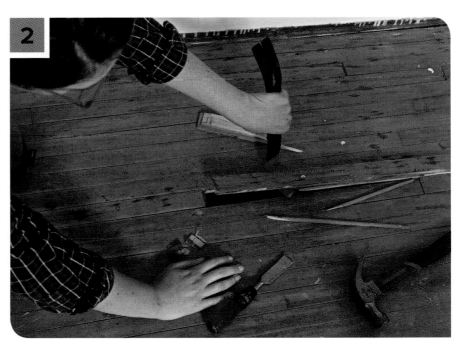

Use a chisel to pry out the flooring pieces, and to complete the cuts at the end of the board so they are smooth. Remove any exposed nails visible in the cutout area.

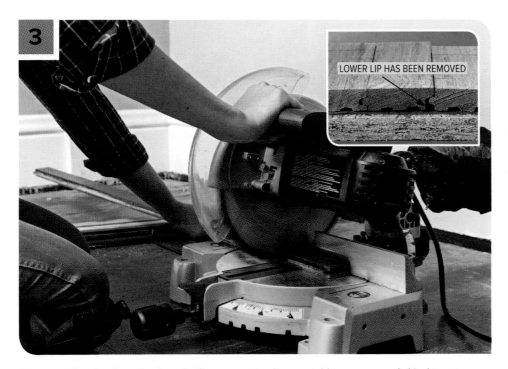

LOWER LIP HAS BEEN REMOVED

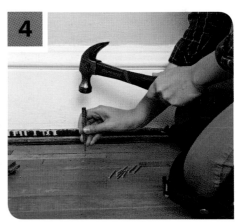

Facenail the new board in place by drilling pilot holes and driving finish nails down through the replacement board and into the subfloor. Recess the nail heads with a nail set, and fill the nail holes with putty. Finish the new board with stain and top coat finish to match the rest of the floor.

Cut a new flooring board to length. Then use a circular saw, table saw, or wood chisel to cut away the bottom lip of the board's groove. Insert the tongue edge of the new board into the groove of the existing board, and lever the board down into place, so that the remaining top groove edge fits over the tongue of the board at the other side of the cutout, as shown in the inset photo.

How to Replace a Section of Hardwood Flooring

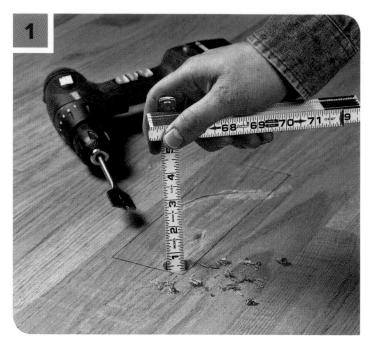

Outline cutting lines around the damaged board. To avoid nails, keep the outline at least ¼" inside the seams between boards. Drill a hole through the damaged board, using a spade bit. Drill until you can see the top of the subfloor. Measure the thickness of the floorboard, then set your circular saw to this depth.

To prevent the boards from chipping, place painter's tape along the outside of the pencil lines. To create a straightedge guide for your saw, tack a straight wood scrap inside the damaged area. Set this straightedge guide back from the cutting line a distance equal to the measurement between the saw blade and the edge of the saw foot plate.

Align the circular saw so the front of the saw foot is against the straightedge guide. Cut along the cutting line, stopping ¼" from the corners. Remove the straightedge guide and repeat along other cutting lines. Complete the cuts with a sharp chisel to loosen the damaged board from the subfloor. For clean cuts, the chisel's beveled side needs to face the damaged area.

Using a pry bar, hammer, and 2 × 4 leverage block, pry up the split board. Remove any nails showing.

5

Use the chisel to remove the narrow strips of remaining wood between the cutout area and the adjoining flooring boards. For a good fit of the replacement board, it is very important to make these cuts as square as possible. Cut a segment of new flooring board to length, then cut away the lower lip of the groove on one side of patch board.

6

Hook the tongue of the replacement piece into the exposed groove of the adjoining old floorboard and use a rubber mallet to tap the groove side down until it is flush with the surrounding floor.

7

On the face of the replacement board, drill pilot holes angled outward at each end, about ½" from the ends. Drive 1½" 8d finish nails into the pilot holes, securing the repair board to the adjoining floorboards. Recess the nail heads with a nail set, and fill the nail holes with wood putty. If there are any gaps along the edges of the replacement piece, also fill them with wood putty. Once the putty is dry, sand the putty and patch area smooth with fine-grit sandpaper. Apply matching wood stain, and let dry; then apply two coats of matching finish.

REPLACING LAMINATE FLOORING

In the event that you need to replace a laminate plank, you must first determine how to remove the damaged plank. If you have a glueless "floating" floor it is best to unsnap and remove each plank starting at the wall and moving in until you reach the damaged plank. However, if the damaged plank is far from the wall, cut out the damaged plank. Fully-bonded laminate planks are secured directly to the underlayment. When you remove the damaged plank, you run the risk of gouging the subfloor, so work with care or call in a professional.

From bottom to top, laminate planks are engineered to resist moisture, scratches, and dents. A melamine base layer protects the inner core layer, which is most often HDF (high-density fiberboard). This is occasionally followed by kraft paper saturated in resins for added protection and durability. The print film is a photographic layer that replicates the look of wood or ceramic. The surface is a highly protective wear layer. The tongue-and-groove planks fit together tightly and may be glued together for added stability.

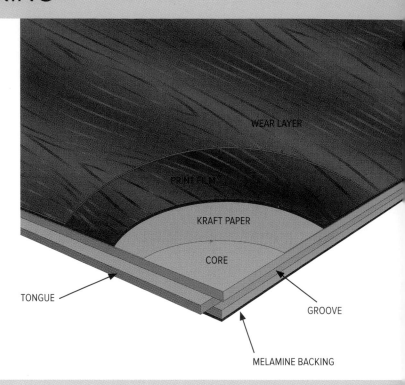

WEAR LAYER

PRINT FILM

KRAFT PAPER

CORE

TONGUE

GROOVE

MELAMINE BACKING

How to Replace Laminate Planks

1

2

Draw a rectangle in the middle of the damaged board with a 1½" border between the rectangle and factory edges. At each rectangle corner and inside each corner of the plank, use a hammer and nail set to make indentations. At each of these indentations, drill ³⁄₁₆" holes into the plank. Only drill the depth of the plank.

To protect the floor from chipping, place painter's tape along the cutlines. Set the circular saw depth to the thickness of the replacement plank. To plunge-cut the damaged plank, slowly lower the saw blade into the cutline until the foot rests flat on the floor. Push the saw from the center of the line out to each end. Stop ¼" in from each corner. Use a hammer to tap a pry bar or chisel into the cutlines. Lift and remove the middle section. Place a sharp chisel between the two drill holes in each corner and strike with a hammer to complete each corner cut. Vacuum.

3

To remove the remaining outer edges of the damaged plank, place a scrap 2 × 4 wood block along the outside of one long cut and use it for leverage to push a pry bar under the flooring. Insert a second pry bar beneath the existing floor (directly under the joint of the adjacent plank) and use a pliers to grab the 1½" border strip in front of the pry bar. Press downward until a gap appears at the joint. Remove the border piece. Remove the opposite strip and then the two short end pieces in the same manner. Remove all of the old glue from the factory edges with a chisel.

4

To remove the tongues on one long and one short end, clamp a straight cutting guide to the replacement plank so the distance from the guide causes the bit to align with the tongue and trim it off. Pressing a router or laminate trimmer against the cutting guide, slowly move along the entire edge of the replacement plank to remove the tongue.

5

6

Set the replacement plank by applying laminate glue to the removed edges of the replacement plank and into the grooves of the existing planks. Firmly press the plank into place. Clean up glue with a damp towel. Place a strip of wax paper over the new plank and evenly distribute some books on the wax paper. Allow the adhesive to dry for 12 to 24 hours.

Dry-fit the grooves on the replacement board into the tongues of the surrounding boards and press into place.

REPAIRING VINYL FLOORING

Repair methods for vinyl flooring depend on the type of floor as well as the type of damage. With sheet vinyl, you can fuse the surface or patch in new material. With vinyl tile, it's best to replace the damaged tiles. Small cuts and scratches can be fused permanently and nearly invisibly with liquid seam sealer, a clear compound that's available wherever vinyl flooring is sold. For tears or burns, the damaged area can be patched. If necessary, remove vinyl from a hidden area, such as the inside of a closet or under an appliance, to use as patch material.

How to Replace Resilient Tile

Use an electric heat gun to warm the damaged tile and soften the underlying adhesive. Keep the heat source moving so you don't melt the tile. When an edge of the tile begins to curl, insert a putty knife to pry up the loose edge until you can remove the tile.

Scrape away remaining adhesive with a putty knife or, for stubborn spots, a floor scraper. Work from the edges to the center so that you don't accidentally scrape up the adjacent tiles. Use mineral spirits to dissolve leftover goop.

When the floor is dry, use a notched trowel—with ⅛" V-shaped notches—held at a 45° angle to apply a thin, even layer of vinyl tile adhesive onto the underlayment.

Set one edge of the tile in place. Lower the tile onto the underlayment and then press it into place. Apply pressure with a J-roller to create a solid bond, starting at the center and working toward the edge to work out air bubbles. If adhesive oozes out the sides, wipe it up with a damp cloth or sponge. Cover the tile with wax paper and some books, and let the adhesive dry for 24 hours.

How to Patch Sheet Vinyl

Measure the width and length of the damaged area. Place the new flooring remnant on a surface you don't mind making some cuts on— like a scrap of plywood. Use a carpenter's square for cutting guidance. Make sure your cutting size is a bit larger than the damaged area.

Lay the patch over the damaged area, matching pattern lines. Secure the patch with duct tape. Using a carpenter's square as a cutting guide, cut through the new vinyl (on top) and the old vinyl (on bottom). Press firmly with the knife to cut both layers.

Remove the damaged section of floor. Work from edges in. When the tile is loosened, insert a putty knife and pry up the damaged material. Scrape off the remaining adhesive with a putty knife or chisel or paint scraper.

Apply adhesive to the patch, using a notched trowel (with ⅛" V-shaped notches) held at a 45° angle to the back of the new vinyl patch.

Set one edge of the patch in place. Lower the patch onto the underlayment. Press into place. Apply pressure with a J-roller or rolling pin to create a solid bond. Start at the center and work toward the edges, working out air bubbles. Let the adhesive dry overnight. Use a soft cloth dipped in lacquer thinner to clean the area. Mix the seam sealer according to the manufacturer's directions.

REPAIRING TILE FLOORS

Although ceramic tile is one of the hardest floorcoverings, it is also fragile and sometimes problems occur. Tiles break and crack. Usually fixing the problem is simply a matter of removing and replacing individual tiles. However, floor movement can cause the adhesive layer beneath the tile to deteriorate. In this case, the adhesive layer must be replaced in order to create an effective, longlasting repair.

Any time you remove tile, check the underlayment. If it's no longer smooth, solid, and level, repair or replace it before replacing the tile. When removing grout or damaged tiles, be careful not to damage surrounding tiles. Always wear eye protection when working with a hammer and chisel. Any time you are doing a major tile installation, make sure to save extra tiles. This way, you will have materials on hand when repairs become necessary.

How to Replace Ceramic Tiles

With a carbide-tipped grout saw, apply firm but gentle pressure across the grout until you expose the unglazed edges of the tile. If the tile is not already cracked, use a hammer to break the tile by tapping a nail set or center punch into the field area. Alternatively, if the tile is significantly cracked, use a chisel to pry up the tile.

Insert a cold chisel into one of the cracks and gently tap the tile. Start at the center and chip outward so you don't damage the adjacent tiles. Be aware that cementboard substrate looks a lot like mortar when you're chiseling. Remove and discard the broken pieces.

3

Use a putty knife to scrape away old thinset adhesive; use a chisel for poured-mortar installation. Once the adhesive is scraped from the underlayment, smooth the rough areas with sandpaper. If there are gouges in the underlayment, fill them with epoxy-based thinset mortar (for cementboard) or a floor-leveling compound (for plywood).

4

Use a notched trowel to apply thinset adhesive to the back of the replacement tile. Set the tile down into the space, doing your best to get it as level as you can with the surrounding tile and to keep it centered in the open area. Use a mallet or hammer and a block of wood covered with cloth or a carpet scrap to lightly tap on the tile, setting it into the adhesive.

5

Use a putty knife to apply grout to the joints. Fill in low spots by applying and smoothing grout with your finger. Use the round edge of a toothbrush handle to create a concave grout line, if desired. Wipe away excess grout with a clean, damp sponge.

REPAIRING CARPET

Burns and stains are the most common carpeting problems. You can clip away the burned fibers of superficial burns using small scissors. Deeper burns and indelible stains require patching by cutting away and replacing the damaged area.

CUSHION-BACK CARPET

Most wall-to-wall carpeting installed today has a stiff, woven backing often made of jute. It is normally installed over a thick carpet pad to create cushion. Other carpet, usually on the more inexpensive side, has a cushion layer bonded to the carpeting permanently. This type of carpet is not stretched so it does not need a kicker or tack strips around the room perimeter. The repair techniques are very similar: you simply remove the damaged area and glue a patch in place.

How to Repair Spot Damage

1

Remove minor damage or stains with a "cookie-cutter" tool, available at carpeting stores. Press the cutter down over the damaged area and twist it to cut away the damaged carpet.

2

Using the cookie-cutter tool again, cut a replacement patch from scrap carpeting. If you did not reserve any, check in a nearby closet for usable, matching material. Insert double-face carpet tape under the cutout, positioning the tape so it overlaps the patch seams.

3

Press the patch into place. Make sure the direction of the nap or pattern matches the existing carpet. To seal the seam and prevent unraveling, apply seam adhesive to the edges of the patch.

How to Restretch Loose Carpet

1

2

Adjust the knob on the head of the knee kicker so the prongs grab the carpet backing without penetrating through the padding. Starting from a corner or near a point where the carpet is firmly attached, press the knee kicker head into the carpet, about 2" from the wall.

Thrust your knee into the cushion of the knee kicker to force the carpet toward the wall. Tuck the carpet edge into the space between the wood strip and the baseboard using a 4" wallboard knife. If the carpet is still loose, trim the edge with a utility knife and stretch it again.

KNEE KICKERS

Knee kickers have teeth that grab the carpet backing. These teeth should be set to grab the backing without grabbing the padding. There is an adjustable knob to do this. You can tell if the knee kicker is grabbing the padding by the increased pressure needed to move it forward. To release the tension just before a damaged area of carpet you intend to patch, place your feet on the floor and use your knee to press it toward the damaged area.

Unless you are planning a major remodeling project, walls and ceiling do not require much attention beyond occasional repair of slight damage and updating of surface with paint or wallcoverings—all common DIY projects. Most often, damage is caused by accidental impact from things like doorknobs or moving furniture. You may also have an occasional nail hole or screw hole to fill, especially if you are redecorating. All of these minor touch ups and repairs are shown in this chapter.

There is, however, another potential cause of damage to walls and ceilings that is less common, but can create huge problems when it makes it presence felt: water. Water can find its way into walls and ceilings through leaky plumbing, clogged and overflowing fixtures, or via leaks in your roofing system. If the source of the water infiltration is caught in time and addressed, damage repair can be limited to cosmetic touch-ups. This is why it is important to keep a close eye on your walls and ceilings for any signs of water—usually indicated by paint blistering or discoloration. Leaks more often are slow and gradual than instantly catastrophic. But the latter can happen, too. Once your wall or ceiling materials (usually drywall these days) become saturated, deterioration is rapid and mold can form quickly. Addressing this type of issue is beyond the scope of a basic home repair book and it is highly recommended that you seek professional home service as soon as possible.

It's a pretty sure bet that once you turn your attention to walls and ceilings, it won't be long before you find yourself on a ladder with a putty knife in your hand.

WALL MAINTENANCE & TOUCH-UPS

Wall maintenance, including washing, should be done on a regular basis, especially in kitchens and bathrooms where grime and humidity are more present. If you are lucky, your kitchen and bathroom walls have a washable surface: this includes most wallcoverings except flat paint, uncoated wallpapers, or delicate paneling. If your kitchen or bathroom wall surfaces are not washable, you should seriously think about upgrading to a gloss paint or vinyl-coated wallpaper, or even ceramic tile.

Most other rooms in your house likely have flat wall paint. This is good from the standpoint that flat paint conceals wall imperfections and is not reflective. But flat paint is very difficult to wash without streaking or altering the finish in a very noticeable way. It is also hard to spot clean.

Wall touch-up/repair materials include self-adhesive seam tape (A); hole-patching kit (B); nail hole filler (C); joint compound (D); stainblocking primer/sealer (E); and sink and tub caulk (F). Some new spackling compounds (G) start out pink and dry white so you can see when they're ready to be sanded and painted. Sponges (H) are useful for smoothing damp joint compound to reduce the amount of sanding that's necessary later.

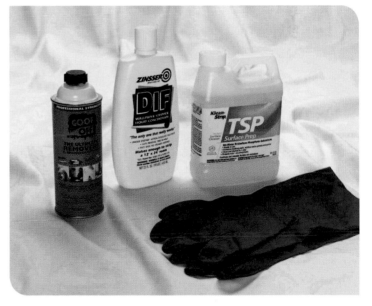

Wall cleaning and degreasing products are needed for both regular maintenance and to prepare walls for paint or wallpaper before a painting project. If wallpaper is to be removed, a wallpaper-removal agent is extremely helpful. Clockwise from top left are cleanup solution to remove old drips and splatters, wallcovering remover to strip old wallcoverings, trisodium phosphate (TSP) for washing the walls, and rubber gloves, which should be worn when using chemicals such as these.

FIXING DRYWALL DAMAGE

Whether in a wall or ceiling, patching holes and concealing popped nails are common drywall repairs. Small holes can be filled directly, but larger patches must be supported with some kind of backing. To repair holes left by nails or screws, dimple the hole slightly with the handle of a utility knife or drywall knife and fill it with spackle or joint compound.

Use joint tape anywhere the drywall's face paper or joint tape has torn or peeled away. Adhesive mesh tapes can make quick work of this, although they can be difficult to get to stick properly. Embedding paper tape in joint compound is more likely to produce satisfactory results but is more time consuming. Always cut away any loose drywall material, face paper, or joint tape from the damaged area, trimming back to solid drywall material.

Large drywall repairs require three coats of joint compound, just like in new installations. Lightly sand your repairs before painting, or adding texture. More minor repairs can usually be accomplished with a one-coat drywall repair compound.

If wallboard is dented, without cracks or tears in the face paper, just fill the hole with lightweight spackling or all-purpose joint compound, let it dry, and sand it smooth.

Most wallboard problems can be remedied with basic wallboard materials and specialty materials: (A) wallboard screws; (B) paper joint tape; (C) self-adhesive fiberglass mesh tape; (D) corner bead; (E) paintable latex or silicone caulk; (F) all-purpose joint compound; (G) lightweight spackling compound; (H) wallboard repair patches; (I) scraps of wallboard; (J) and wallboard repair clips.

To repair a popped nail, drive a wallboard screw 2" above or below the nail, so it pulls the panel tight to the framing. Scrape away loose paint or compound, then drive the popped nail 1/16" below the surface. Apply joint compound to cover the holes.

How to Repair Cracks & Gashes

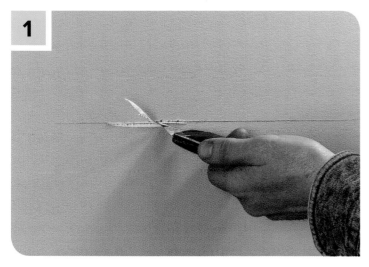

1

Use a utility knife to cut away loose drywall or face paper and widen the crack into a "V"; the notch will help hold the joint compound.

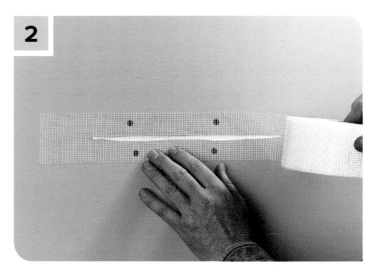

2

Push along the sides of the crack with your hand. If the drywall moves, secure the panel with 1¼" drywall screws driven into the nearest framing members. Cover the crack and screws with self-adhesive mesh tape.

3

Cover the tape with compound, lightly forcing it into the mesh, then smooth it off, leaving just enough to conceal the tape. Add two more coats, in successively broader and thinner coats to blend the patch into the surrounding area.

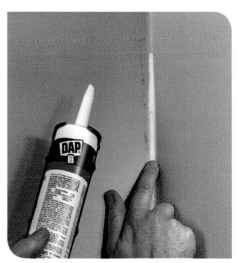

OPTION: For small cracks at corners, apply a thin bead of paintable latex or silicone caulk over the crack, then use your finger to smooth the caulk into the corner.

How to Patch Small Holes in Drywall

1

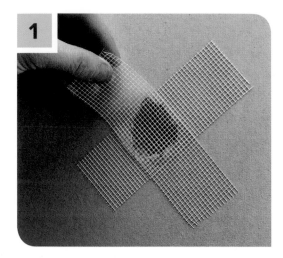

Trim away any broken drywall, face paper, or joint tape around the hole, using a utility knife. Cover the hole with crossed strips of self-adhesive mesh tape.

2

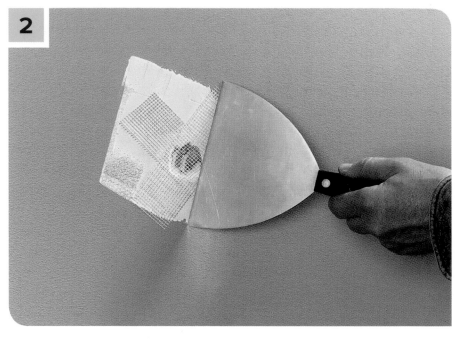

Cover the tape with all-purpose joint compound, lightly forcing it into the mesh, then smooth it off, leaving just enough to conceal the tape.

3

Add two more coats of compound in successively broader and thinner coats to blend the patch into the surrounding area. Use a drywall wet sander to smooth the repair area.

How to Patch Large Holes in Drywall

1

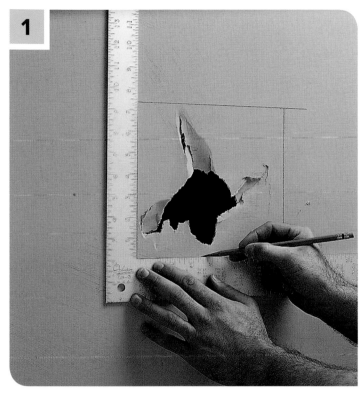

Outline the damaged area, using a framing square. (Cutting four right angles makes it easier to measure and cut the patch.) Use a drywall saw to cut along the outline.

2

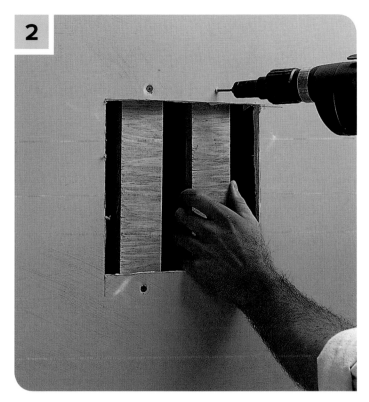

Cut plywood or lumber backer strips a few inches longer than the height of the cutout. Fasten the strips to the back side of the drywall, drilling through the front with 1¼" drywall screws.

3

Cut a drywall patch ⅛" smaller than the cutout dimensions, and fasten it to the backer strips with screws. Apply mesh joint tape over the seams. Finish the seams with three coats of compound.

REPAIRING PLASTER

Plaster walls, common before the 1950s but somewhat rare these days, are created by building up layers of plaster to form a hard, durable wall surface. Behind the plaster itself is a gridlike layer of wood, metal, or rock lath that holds the plaster in place. Keys, formed when the base plaster is squeezed through the lath, hold the dried plaster to the ceiling or walls.

Before you begin any plaster repair, make sure the surrounding area is in good shape. If the lath is deteriorated or the plaster is soft, call a professional.

Use a latex bonding liquid to ensure a good bond and a tight, crack-free patch. Bonding liquid also eliminates the need to wet the plaster and lath to prevent premature drying and shrinkage, which could ruin the repair.

Spackle is used to conceal cracks, gashes, and small holes in plaster. Some new spackling compounds start out pink and dry white so you can see when they're ready to be sanded and painted. Use lightweight spackle for low-shrinkage and one-application fills.

How to Fill Dents & Small Holes in Plaster

1

Scrape or sand away any loose plaster or peeling paint to establish a solid base for the new plaster.

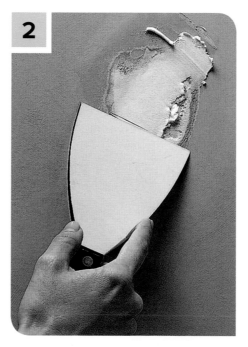

2

Fill the hole with lightweight spackle. Apply the spackle with the smallest knife that will span the damaged area. Let the spackle dry, following the manufacturer's instructions.

3

Sand the patch lightly with 150-grit sandpaper. Wipe the dust away with a clean cloth, then prime and paint the area, feathering the paint to blend the edges.

How to Patch Large Holes in Plaster

1

Sand or scrape any texture or loose paint from the area around the hole to create a smooth, firm edge. Use a wallboard knife to test the plaster around the edges of the damaged area. Scrape away all loose or soft plaster.

2

Mix patching plaster as directed by the manufacturer, and use a wallboard knife or trowel to apply it to the hole. Fill shallow holes with a single coat of plaster. For deeper holes, apply a shallow first coat, then scratch a crosshatch pattern in the wet plaster (inset photo). Let it dry, then apply a second coat of plaster. Let the plaster dry, and sand it lightly.

How to Repair Cracks in Plaster

1

Scrape away any texture or loose plaster around the crack. Using a utility knife, cut back the edges of the crack to create a "keyway" along the crack so the repair product can get far enough in to stay in place.

2

Work joint compound into the keyway using a 6" knife, then embed mesh tape into the compound, lightly forcing the compound through the mesh. Smooth the compound, leaving just enough to conceal the tape.

3

Add two more coats of compound, in successively broader and thinner coats, to blend the patch into the surrounding area. Lightly sand, then retexture the repair area to match the wall. Prime and paint it to finish the repair.

A sure sign of a water problem is discoloration and bubbling on the ceiling surface. Water from a leaky roof or pipe above will quickly find a low spot or a joint between drywall panels, soaking through to the visible surface. Water in joints is especially damaging because it ruins the edges of two panels at once. If you have a water problem, be sure to fix the leak and allow the damaged drywall to dry thoroughly before making any repairs.

Whenever water or moisture infiltrates a house, there is always a concern regarding mold. Mold grows where water and nutrients are present—damp wallboard paper can provide such an environment. You can use a damp rag and baking soda or a small amount of detergent to clean up small areas of mold (less than 1 square yard), though you should wear goggles, rubber gloves, and a dust mask to prevent contact with mold spores. If mold occupies more area than this, you may have a more serious problem. Contact a mold abatement specialist for assessment and remediation. To help prevent mold growth, use exhaust fans and dehumidifiers to rid your home of excess moisture and repair plumbing leaks as soon as they are found.

How to Repair Water-Damaged Drywall

1

After the source for the water leak has been fixed, cut 4" holes at each end of joist and stud bays to help ventilation. Where possible, remove wet or damp insulation to dry out. Use fans and dehumidifiers to help speed up the drying process.

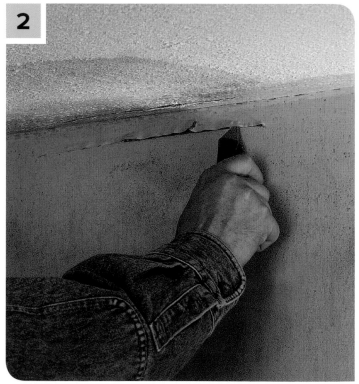

2

Remove loose tape and compound using a utility knife. Cut back areas of soft drywall to solid material. To prevent sagging, prop waterlogged ceiling panels against joists with "T" braces (a ceiling-height 2 × 4 with a 2 × 4 crosspiece attached to the top).

3

Once drywall is dry, refasten ceiling panels to framing or remove panels that are excessively bowed. Reinforce damaged wall panels with drywall screws driven 2" from the existing fasteners.

4

Patch all vent holes and damaged areas with drywall (see pages 32 to 35) and replace any insulation. Apply a quality stain-blocking primer/sealer to the affected area. Use an oil-based sealer; latex-based sealers may allow water stains to bleed through.

5

After the primer/sealer has dried, finish all joints and repairs with paper tape and three coats of compound. If water stains bleed through, reseal prior to final priming and painting.

REPAIRING WALLCOVERINGS

Loosened seams and bubbles are common wallcovering problems, but both are easy to remedy using a little adhesive and a sponge. For papers that are compatible with water, use a clean, damp sponge. For other types of papers (grasscloth or flocked wallcoverings, for example), clean fingers are probably the best choice.

Scratches, tears, or obvious stains can be patched so successfully that the patch is difficult to spot. Whenever you hang wallcoverings, save remnants for future repairs. It's also a good idea to record the name of the manufacturer as well as the style and run numbers of the wallcoverings. Write this information on a piece of masking tape and put it on the back of a switchplate in the room.

If you need to patch an area of wallcovering but don't have remnants available, you can remove a section of wallcovering from an inconspicuous spot, such as inside a closet or behind a door. You can camouflage the spot by painting the hole with a color that blends into the background of the wallcovering.

How to Fix a Bubble

Cut a slit through the bubble, using a sharp utility knife. If there is a pattern in the wallcovering, cut along a line in the pattern to hide the slit.

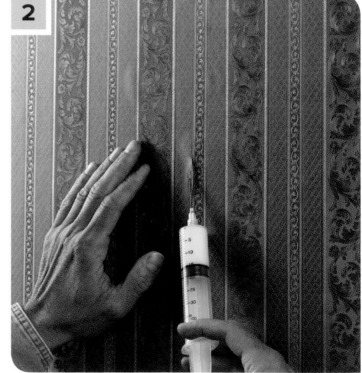

Insert the tip of a glue applicator through the slit and apply adhesive sparingly to the wall under the wallcovering. Press the wallcovering gently to rebond it. Use a clean, damp sponge to press the flap down and wipe away excess glue.

How to Patch Wallcoverings

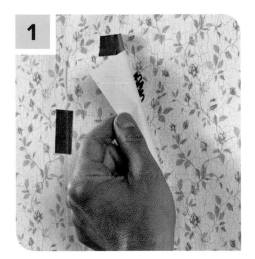

Fasten a scrap of matching wallcovering over the damaged portion with low-adhesive tape, so that the patterns match.

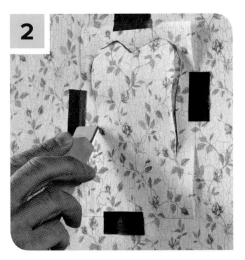

Holding a utility knife blade at a 90° angle to the wall, cut through both layers of wallcovering. If the wallcovering has strong pattern lines, cut along the lines to hide the seams. With less definite patterns, cut irregular lines.

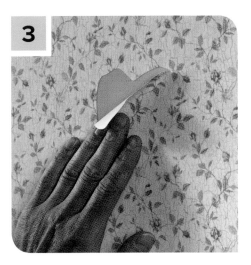

Remove the scrap and patch, then peel away the damaged wallcovering. Apply adhesive to the back of the patch and position it in the hole so that the pattern matches. Rinse the patch area with a damp sponge.

How to Remove Wallcovering

Find a loose edge and try to strip off the wallcovering. Vinyls often peel away easily. If the wallcovering does not strip by hand, cover the floor with layers of newspaper. Add wallcovering remover fluid to a bucket of water, as directed by the manufacturer.

Pierce the wallcovering surface with a wallpaper scorer, sometimes called a tiger claw (inset) to allow remover solution to enter and soften the adhesive. Use a pressure sprayer, paint roller, or sponge to apply the remover solution. Let it soak into the covering, according to the manufacturer's directions.

Peel away loosened wallcovering with a 6" wallboard knife. Be careful not to damage the plaster or wallboard. Remove all backing paper. Rinse adhesive residue from the wall with remover solution or TSP. Rinse with clear water and let the walls dry completely.

Ceramic tile is durable and nearly maintenance free, but like every other material in your house, it can fail or develop problems. The most common problem with ceramic tile involves damaged or discolored grout. Failed grout is unattractive, but the real danger is that it offers a point of entry for water. Given a chance to work its way beneath grout, water can destroy a tile base and eventually wreck an entire installation. It's important to regrout ceramic tile as soon as you see signs of damage.

Another potential problem for tile installations is damaged caulk. In tub and shower stalls and around sinks and backsplashes, the joints between the tile and the fixtures are sealed with caulk. The caulk eventually deteriorates, leaving an entry point for water. Unless the joints are recaulked, seeping water can destroy the tile base and the wall.

How to Regrout Wall Tile

Use an awl or utility knife to scrape out the old grout completely, leaving a clean bed for the new grout. You can also use a grout saw (see page 24).

Clean and rinse the grout joints, then spread grout over the entire tile surface, using a rubber grout float or sponge. Work the grout well into the joints and let it set slightly.

Wipe away excess grout with a damp sponge. When the grout is dry, wipe away the residue and polish the tiles with a dry cloth.

How to Recaulk a Tub/Shower Seal

1

Start with a completely dry surface. Scrape out the old caulk and clean the joint with a cloth dipped in rubbing alcohol. This can be time-consuming, but take care to get as much old material out as you can.

2

Cut the tip off caulk cartridges at a 45° angle and then make a flat cut at the top with a utility knife. This will allow you to deliver a smooth bead that is not too thin or too heavy. Fill the joint with silicone or latex caulk. Pros can lay a perfect bead, but for most DIYers you'll get better, more attractive results if you wet your fingertip with cold water, then use your finger to smooth the caulk into a cove shape.

How to Remove & Replace a Broken Wall Tile

1

Carefully scrape away the grout from the surrounding joints, using a utility knife, awl, or grout saw. Break the damaged tile into small pieces, using a hammer and chisel. Remove the broken pieces, then scrape away debris or old adhesive from the open area.

2

Test-fit the replacement tile and make sure it sits flush with the field. Spread adhesive on the back of the replacement tile and place it in the hole, twisting it slightly. Use masking tape to hold the tile in place for 24 hours so the adhesive can dry. Remove the tape, then apply premixed grout, using a sponge or grout float

REPAIRING CEILINGS

Most ceiling repairs are relatively simple: the techniques used to repair wallboard walls apply to ceilings as well, while sagging panels can be refastened or replaced easily; the edges of acoustical tiles make it easy to remove and replace a single tile; and textures can be matched with a little practice on a scrap of cardboard or simply removed altogether.

However, plaster, by contrast, is difficult to work with, and replastering is not an option for most homeowners. While minor repairs are manageable, widespread failure can be dangerous. If you find large spongy areas or extensive sags consult a professional.

Removing ceiling texture is not really a home repair, but it something many homeowners want to do so they can replace the texture with a more modern home décor product. It is a messy job, but generally the texture comes off pretty easily. Spray the textured area with a light detergent, wait a half hour or so, and then start scraping with a 6" drywall knife. Patch any damaged areas with joint compound, then prime and paint.

How to Raise a Sagging Wallboard Ceiling

1

Remove loose tape and compound at joints between loose panels. Starting at one end, drive wallboard screws with broad, thin washers every 4" through the center of the joint and into the joists. In the field of panel, drive screws 2" from existing fasteners.

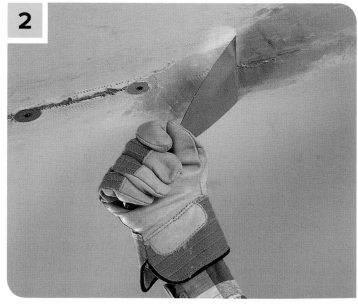

2

When the area is securely fastened, scrape off any loose chips of paint or wallboard around joints and screws, then fill with compound. Cover large cracks or gaps with fiberglass tape before applying the compound.

How to Replace Acoustical Ceiling Tile

Cut out the center section of the damaged tile with a utility knife. Slide the edges away from the surrounding tiles.

Trim the upper lip of the grooved edges of the new tile, using a straightedge. If necessary, also remove one of the tongues.

At the ceiling, apply construction adhesive to the furring strips. Install the new tile, tongue first, and press it into the adhesive.
TIP: To hold large tiles in place while the glue dries, place a flat board across the tile, then wedge a 2 × 4 post between the board and the floor.

VARIATION:

Because acoustical tiles are attached directly to a grid of supports, often wood, replacing them is more challenging than replacing a suspended ceiling tile. Suspended ceiling tiles are simply dry-fitted into a support network of metal tracks, and there is usually enough space above them to manipulate them enough to get a bad one out and a new one in. Handle the tiles carefully, they are a bit fragile—especially around the edges.

PAINTING WALLS & CEILINGS

Painting interior walls and ceilings is one of the projects most DIYers think they know how to do correctly, and perhaps for this reason it is the first home improvement project most new homeowners tackle. And to some extent, DIYers are right. Indoor painting is basically a three-step process:

1. **Preparation.** Clean surfaces (see pages 29 to 31), remove trim moldings, apply masking tape around window and door frames. Protect the floor. Also be sure to provide good ventilation and lighting and the working area clear by moving furniture to another room.

2. **Product selection.** This applies not only to paints and primers but to your application tools and cleanup products as well.

3. **Application.** Whether you are using brushes, rollers, sponges, or even power sprayers, follow these tips: Work from high to low; Overlap you application swaths by at least 6 inches; Apply two or more thin coats of paint, not one thick coat.

LADDER SAFETY

Ladder safety is of course a very important consideration when working high on your walls or on your ceiling. Don't skimp on quality—most rental centers have a full assortment of ladders and scaffolding for reasonable rental rates. Two quality stepladders and an extension plank are all you need to paint most interior surfaces, including ceilings. For painting high areas, build a simple scaffold by running the plank through the steps of two stepladders. It can be easy to lose your balance or step off the plank, so choose tall ladders for safety. Buy a strong, straight 2" × 10" board no more than 10 feet long, or rent a plank from a material dealer or rental outlet.

Some painting projects require special preparation, which can include the application of specialty products. Primarily, these include painting old surfaces that are not smooth, as when you remove wallpaper (see page 39), or very glossy surfaces, such as enamel paint, that require deglossing for the new paint to stick.

Tips for Painting Walls and Ceilings

Fresh, unpainted drywall should be primed with a high-quality drywall primer.

Don't overload a paint brush. Dip it into the paint, loading one third of its bristle length. Tap the bristles against the side of the can to remove excess paint, but do not drag the bristles against the lip of the can.

Paint to a wet edge. Cut in the edges on small sections with a paint-brush, then immediately roll the section. Using a corner roller makes it unnecessary to cut in inside corners. With two painters, have one cut in with a brush while the other rolls the large areas.

Minimize brush marks. Slide the roller cover slightly off of the roller cage when rolling near wall corners or a ceiling line. Brushed areas dry to a different finish than rolled paint.

WINDOWS & DOORS

It should be no great surprise that windows and doors require more maintenance than other buildings in your house. For one, they move and are subjected to the stresses of opening, closing, slamming, and more. And they are also exposed directly to the elements: not just on the exterior, but in the critical heating and cooling envelope that surrounds the walls of your home. There, drastic changes in temperature and humidity can cause a host of issues.

Maintaining windows and doors has changed as a pursuit in the past few decades. Not so long ago, if a window broke it was down to the basement to fetch the glazing compound and glazier's compound to secure the replacement window glass in the opening. Today, most of the important windows in the modern home are not simple glass panes, but are sealed sandwiches of glass and gas called Insulated Glass Units (IGU). If one of those breaks, there is a little a homeowner can do to repair it other than buy a new IGU and try to install it, which can easily cost as much as replacing an entire window.

If your window was sticking or opening and closing roughly, the problem in the old days was likely to be the system of window sash counterweights, cords, and pulleys inside the wall next to the window. Today's opening and closing mechanisms are integral to the window unit, usually involving springloaded mechanisms captured in the frame: easier to fix than IGUs, but often hard to get at and modern vinyl cladding does not always hold up to home repair.

Doors have not changed as much mechanically, but they have changed a lot materially. Few doors are wood any longer. Most exterior doors are made of steel filled with foam insulation or with fiberglass. Interior doors are just as likely to be made entirely of synthetic polymers as they are to be wood.

The upshot is, maintaining and repairing modern windows and doors is mostly a matter of understanding how they are built and which kinds of improvements are achievable.

Window and door repairs fall into two basic categories: improving operation and upgrading weatherization.

Modern entry doors are more accurately described as entry systems. Most are shipped prehung, often with transoms and sidelites preinstalled. This simplifies installation—you simply tip it up into the door opening and screw it in place. But it complicates getting at the parts and limits what you can do as far as repair and maintenance.

Door hardware, too, is changing constantly, often for stylistic reasons. The sliding barn-door hardware seen here is a good example. It is relatively simple, but keeping up with technological door and window hardware advances can require some attention,

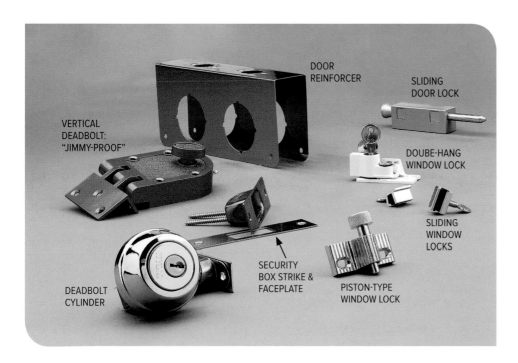

DOOR REINFORCER

SLIDING DOOR LOCK

VERTICAL DEADBOLT: "JIMMY-PROOF"

DOUBE-HANG WINDOW LOCK

SLIDING WINDOW LOCKS

DEADBOLT CYLINDER

SECURITY BOX STRIKE & FACEPLATE

PISTON-TYPE WINDOW LOCK

Window and door security remains an issue that most homeowners have the capacity to improve-not just with mechanical additions, but by instituting safer practices and my taking advantage of the growing list of app-based products that assist in home monitoring. The relatively simple products seen at left are all effective and easy to install.

FIXING COMMON DOOR PROBLEMS

Many door problems are caused by loose hinges. When hinges are loose, the door won't hang right, causing it to rub and stick and throw off the latch mechanism. The first thing to do is check the hinge screws. If the holes for the hinge screws are worn and won't hold the screws, try the repair on the next page. If the hinges are tight but the door still rubs against the frame, sand or plane down the door's edge. Door latch problems can occur for a number of other reasons, including door warpage, swollen wood, sticking latchbolts, and paint buildup. If you've addressed those issues and the door still won't stay shut, it's probably because the door frame is out of square. This happens as a house settles with age; you can make minor adjustments by filing the strike plate on the door frame. If there's some room between the frame and the door, you can align the latchbolt and strike plate by shimming the hinges. Or, drive a couple of extra-long screws to pull the frame into adjustment.

Common closet doors, such as sliding and bifold types, usually need only some minor adjustments and lubrication to stay in working order.

Door locksets tend to be very reliable, but they do need to be cleaned and lubricated occasionally. One simple way to keep an entry door lockset working smoothly is to spray a light lubricant into the keyhole, then move the key in and out a few times. Don't use graphite in locksets, as it can abrade some metals with repeated use.

STICKING DOORS

Sticking doors usually leave a mark where they rub against the door frame. Warped doors may resist closing and feel springy when you apply pressure. Check for warpage with a straightedge.

Draw pencil lines across the wear areas and sand until the marks disappear. Recheck and repeat if necessary.

How to Remove a Door

1 Drive the lower hinge pin out using a screwdriver and hammer. Have a helper hold the door in place, then drive out the upper (and center, if applicable) hinge pins. Once you have the hinge pin started, you may find it easier to extract it with pliers.

2 Remove the door and set it aside. Clean and lubricate the hinge pins before reinstalling the door.

How to Tighten a Loose Hinge Plate

1 Remove the door from the hinges. Tighten any loose screws on the door jamb or the door itself. If the wood won't hold the screws tightly, remove all the hinge plate screws to access the screw holes.

2 Coat wooden golf tees or wood dowels with wood glue, and drive them into the worn screw holes. If necessary, drill out the screw holes to accept dowels—it's better than pounding too hard on the dee or dowels and splitting the jamb wood. Let the glue dry, then cut off excess wood with a sharp utility knife.

3 Drill small pilot holes in the new wood patch, and reinstall the hinge.

Tips for Aligning a Latchbolt & Strike Plate

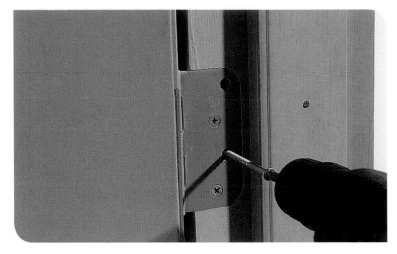

Install a thin cardboard shim behind the bottom hinge to raise the position of the latchbolt. To lower the latchbolt, shim behind the top hinge. Reinstall the hinge plate.

Remove two hinge screws from the top or bottom hinge, and drive a 3" wood screw into each hole. The screws will reach the framing studs in the wall and pull the door jamb, changing the angle of the door. Add long screws to the top hinge to raise the latchbolt or to the bottom hinge to lower it.

Tips for Straightening a Warped Door

Adjust the door trim to follow the door. You can do this by removing or loosening the doorstop molding and reattaching it to conform to the door's warped profile. You likely will have some touch-up work to do on the door jamb where the doorstop edge has moved.

If the warpage is slight, you may be able to straighten it by removing it and placing heavy weights on the convex side of the warpage. Leave the weights on the door for several days, and check it periodically with a straightedge. This has a relatively low chance of success but may be worth a try.

Tips for Freeing a Sticking Door

Tighten all of the hinge screws. If the door still sticks, use light pencil lines to mark the areas where the door rubs against the door jamb. Remove the door and sand the sticking points. You may be able to get away with sanding the door while it is still hanging. Replace the door and test the fit. If the sanding has not fixed the sticking, remove it again and go to the next step.

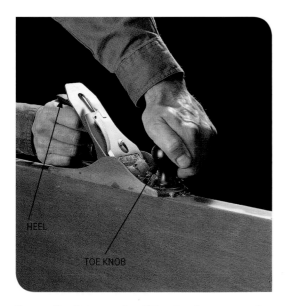

HEEL

TOE KNOB

Secure the door on-edge. If the door has veneered surfaces, sand back the veneer edges slightly so they do not catch the plane blade and splinter. Grip the toe knob and handle firmly, and plane with long, smooth strokes. You could also use a belt sander or a power planer for this step if you are not good with a hand plane—it is an acquired skill. Check the door's fit, then sand the planed area smooth.

Apply clear sealer or paint to the sanded or planed area and any other exposed surfaces of the door. This will prevent moisture from entering the wood and is especially important for entry doors.

Tips for Sliding Doors

MOUNTING SCREW

Clean the tracks above and below the doors with a toothbrush and a damp cloth or a hand vacuum. Spray a greaseless lubricant on all the rollers, but do not spray the tracks. Replace any bent or worn parts.

Check the gap along the bottom edge of the door to make sure it is even. To adjust the gap, rotate the mounting screw to raise or lower the door edge.

Tips for Bifold Doors

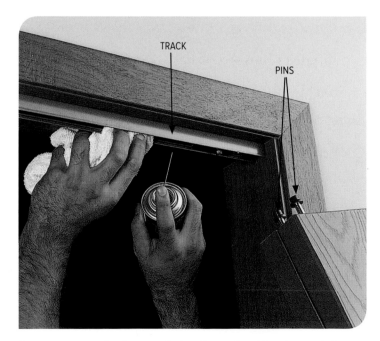

TRACK

PINS

PIVOT BLOCK

Open or remove the doors and wipe the tracks with a clean rag. Spray the tracks and rollers or pins with greaseless lubricant.

Check closed doors for alignment within the door frame. If the gap between the closed doors is uneven, adjust the top pivot blocks with a screwdriver or wrench.

How to Shorten a Hollow-core Door

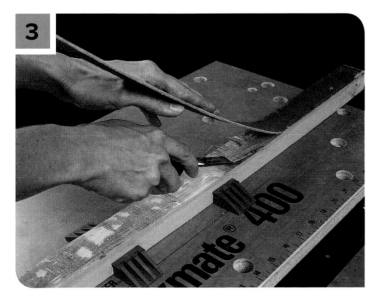

Mark the cutting line. Cut through the door veneer with a sharp utility knife to prevent it from chipping when the door is sawed.

Lay the door on sawhorses and clamp a straightedge to the door as a cutting guide. Saw off the bottom of the door. The hollow core of the door may be exposed.

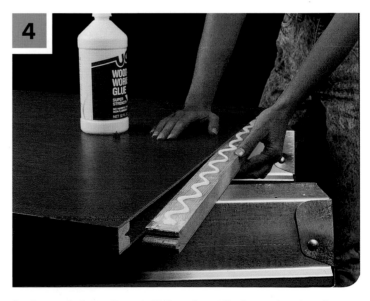

To reinstall a cutoff frame piece in the bottom of the door, remove the frame piece from the door and chisel the veneer from both sides of the frame.

Apply wood glue to the cutoff piece. Insert the frame piece into the opening at the door bottom and clamp it. Wipe away any excess glue and let the glue dry overnight.

FIXING COMMON WINDOW PROBLEMS

Many of us have experienced difficulty with opening windows due to swollen wood or painted channels. Almost as frequent, windows won't stay open because of a broken sash cord (on very old windows) or failed spring-load device. Double-hung windows with spring-loaded sash tracks require cleaning and an occasional adjustment of the springs in (or behind) the tracks. Casement windows are often faulty at the crank mechanisms. If cleaning doesn't fix the problem, the crank mechanism must be replaced.

Spring-lift windows operate with the help of a spring-loaded lift rod inside a metal tube. Adjust them by unscrewing the top end of the tube from the jamb, then twisting the tube to change the spring tension: clockwise for more lifting power; counterclockwise for less. Maintain a tight grip on the tube at all times to keep it from unwinding.

Windows endure temperature extremes, house settling, and all sorts of wear and tear. Sooner or later, you'll need to perform a bit of maintenance to keep them working properly.

Spring-loaded windows have an adjustment screw on the track insert. Adjust both sides until the window is balanced and opens and closes smoothly.

Tips for Freeing Stuck Windows

Cut the paint film if the window is painted shut. Insert a paint zipper (the tool seen above, sold at most hardware stores) or utility knife between the window stop and the sash, and slide it down to break the seal.

Place a block of scrap wood against the window sash. Tap *very lightly* with a hammer to free the window.

Lubricate window channels by rubbing them with a white candle, then opening and closing the window a few times. Do not use liquid lubricants on wood windows

How to Lubricate Casement Window Cranks

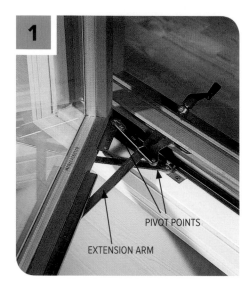

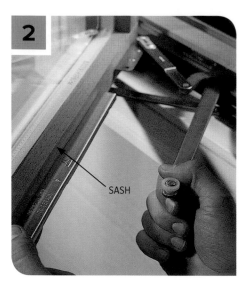

PIVOT POINTS

EXTENSION ARM

SASH

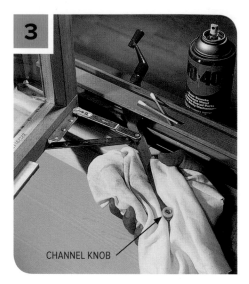

CHANNEL KNOB

If a casement window is hard to crank, clean the accessible parts. Open the window until the roller at the end of the extension arm is aligned with the access slot in the window track.

Disengage the extension arm by pulling it down and out of the track. Clean the track with a stiff brush, and wipe the pivoting arms and hinges with a rag.

Lubricate the track and hinges with spray lubricant or household oil. Wipe off excess lubricant with a cloth, then reattach the extension arm. If that doesn't solve the problem, repair or replace the crank assembly.

How to Repair a Casement Window Crank Assembly

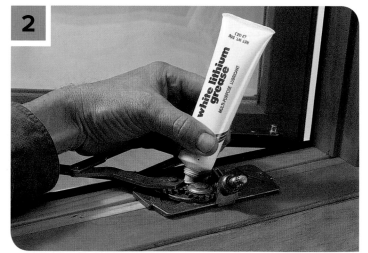

Disengage the extension arm from the window track, then remove the molding or cap concealing the crank mechanism. Unhinge any pivot arms connected to the window. Remove the screws securing the crank assembly, then remove the assembly and clean it thoroughly. If the gears are badly worn, replace the assembly. Check a home center or contact the manufacturer for new parts. Note which way the window opens—to the right or left—when ordering replacement parts.

Apply an all-purpose grease to the gears, and reinstall the assembly. Connect the pivot arms, and attach the extension arm to the window. Test the window operation before installing the cap and molding.

How to Replace Window Glass

1

2

Wearing heavy leather gloves, remove the broken pieces of glass. Then, soften the old glazing compound using a heat gun or a hair dryer (carefully). Scrape out softened putty with a putty knife. If a section is difficult to scrape clean, reheat it.

Apply a thin bed of glazing compound to the wood frame opening and smooth it in place with your thumb. If you are having trouble getting the glazing compound to stick, make sure the product is not too old and dried out—fresh compound always works better. You can also try applying a coat of shellac on the wood in the recess if the wood frame is very old.

3

4

Make a rope of glazing compound (about ½" dia.) by rolling it between your hands. Then press it against the pane and the wood frame. Smooth it in place by drawing a putty knife, held at a 45° angle, across its surface. Scrape off excess. Let the glazing compound dry for at least one week, and then prime and paint it to match the rest of the sash. When the paint is dry, scrape off the extra with a razor blade paint scraper.

Press the new pane into the opening, making sure to achieve a tight seal with the compound on all sides. Do not press all the compound out. Drive glazier's points into the wood frame to hold the pane in place. Use the tip of a putty knife to slide the point against the surface of the glass. Install at least two points on each side of the pane.

No matter whether you live in a hot or a cold climate, weatherizing your home's windows and doors can pay off handsomely. Heating and cooling costs may account for over half of the total household energy bill. Since most weatherizing projects are relatively inexpensive, you can recover your investment quickly. In fact, in some climates, you can pay back the cost of a weatherproofing project in one season.

If you live in a cold climate, you probably already understand the importance of weatherizing. The value of keeping warm air inside the house during a cold winter is obvious. From the standpoint of energy efficiency, it's equally important to prevent warm air from entering the house during summer.

Weatherizing your home is an ideal do-it-yourself project, because it can be done a little at a time, according to your schedule. In cold climates, the best time of the year to weatherize is the fall, before it turns too cold to work outdoors.

Generally, metal and metal-reinforced weather stripping is more durable than products made of plastic, rubber, or foam. However, even plastic, rubber, and foam weather stripping products have a wide range of quality. The best rubber products are those made from neoprene rubber—use this whenever it's available.

Weatherizing products commonly found in home centers include clear film, heat-shrink window insulator kit (A); an aluminum door threshold with vinyl weather stripping insert (B); a nail-on, rubber door sweep (C); minimal expanding spray foam (D); silicone window and door caulk (E); open-cell foam caulk-backer rod (F); self-adhesive, closed-cell foam weather stripping coil (G); flexible brass weather stripping coil, also called V-channel, (H).

Tips for Weatherizing Windows & Doors

Caulking is a simple and inexpensive way to fill narrow gaps, indoors or out. One primary spot for heat loss is the gap between the window brickmold and the exterior wall.

A felt, bristle, or rubber door sweep seals out drafts, even if you have an uneven floor or a low threshold.

Install a storm door to decrease drafts and energy loss through entry doors. Look for an insulated storm door with a continuous hinge and seamless exterior surface.

Patio door: Use rubber compression strips to seal the channels in patio door jambs, where movable panels fit when closed. Also install a patio door insulator kit (plastic sheeting installed similarly to plastic sheeting for windows) on the interior side of the door.

Cut two pieces of metal tension strip or V-channel the full height of the door opening, and cut another to full width. Use wire brads to tack the strips to the door jambs and door header on the interior side of the doorstops. Attach metal weather stripping from the top down to help prevent buckling. Flare out the tension strips with a putty knife to fill the gaps between the jambs and the door when the door is in the closed position (do not pry too far at a time).

Sliding windows: Treat side-by-side sliding windows as if they were double-hung windows turned 90°. For greater durability, use metal tension strips, rather than self-adhesive compressible foam, in the sash track that fit against the edge of the sash when the window is closed.

Add reinforced felt strips to the edge of the doorstop on the exterior side. The felt edge should form a close seal with the door when closed. Drive fasteners only until they are flush with the surface of the reinforcing spine—overdriving will cause damage and buckling.

Casement windows: Attach self-adhesive foam or rubber compression strips on the outside edges of the window stops.

Storm windows: Create a tight seal by attaching foam compression strips to the outside of storm window stops. After installing the storm window, fill any gaps between the exterior window trim and the storm window with caulk backer rope.

Lower sash of a double-hung window. Wipe down the underside of the bottom window sash with a damp rag, and let it dry; then attach self-adhesive compressible foam or rubber to the underside of the sash. Use high-quality hollow neoprene strips, if available. This will create an airtight seal when the window is locked in position.

BOTTOM SASH (RAISED)

TOP SASH (LOWERED)

Upper sash of a double-hung window. Seal the gap between the top sash and the bottom sash on double-hung windows. Lift the bottom sash and lower the top sash to improve access, and tack metal V-channel to the bottom rail of the top sash using wire brads. The open end of the "V" should be pointed downward so moisture cannot collect in the channel. Flare out the V-channel with a putty knife to fit the gap between the sash.

Compared to removable wood storm windows and screens, repairing combination storm windows is a little more complex. The metal-frame combination windows reside not just in window openings but in the glazing of full-height storm doors as well. But there are several repairs you can make without too much difficulty, as long as you find the right parts. Take the old corner keys, gaskets, or other original parts to a hardware store that repairs storm windows so the clerk can help you find the correct replacement parts. If you cannot find the right parts, have a new sash built.

RELEASE TAB

Remove the metal storm window sash by pressing in the release hardware in the lower rail then lifting the sash out. Sash hangers on the corners of the top rail should be aligned with the notches in the side channels before removal.

How to Replace Screening in a Metal Storm Window

1

2

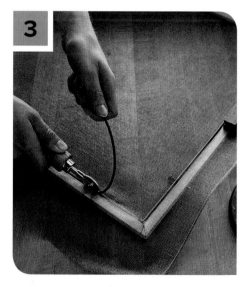

3

Pry the vinyl spline from the groove around the edge of the frame with a screwdriver. Retain the old spline if it is still flexible, otherwise replace it with a new spline.

Stretch the new screening tightly over the frame so that it overlaps the edges of the frame. Keeping the screen taut, use the convex side of a spline roller to press the screen into the retaining grooves.
TIP: You can have insect screening, mostly fiberglass these days, cut to size at most hardware stores, or you may be able to purchase it from a roll by the lineal foot. Make sure your replacement screening is at least 6" larger than the window frame in both directions.

Use the concave side of the spline roller (a specialty item available at hardware stores specifically for this purpose) to press the spline into the groove—it helps to have a partner for this. Carefully cut away excess screening using a sharp utility knife and a straightedge to hold the screening tight against the frame.
CAUTION: The screening is prone to catching on the blade and being torn from the retaining grooves if it is not taut.

How to Replace Glass in a Metal Storm Window

Remove the sash frame from the window, then completely remove the broken glass from the sash (wear heavy gloves). Remove the rubber gasket that framed the old glass pane and remove any glass remnants. Find the dimensions for the replacement glass by measuring between the inside edges of the frame opening, then adding twice the thickness of the rubber gasket to each measurement.

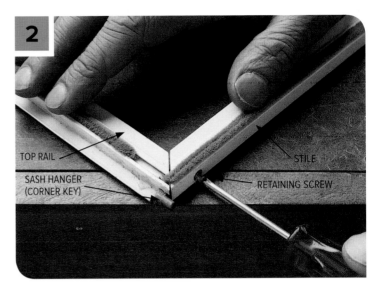

Set the frame on a flat surface, and disconnect the top rail. Remove the retaining screws in the sides of the frame stiles where they join the top rail. After unscrewing the retaining screws, pull the top rail loose, pulling gently in a downward motion to avoid damaging the L-shaped corner keys that join the rail and the stiles. For glass replacement, you need disconnect only the top rail.

Fit the rubber gasket (buy a replacement if the original is in poor condition) around one edge of the replacement glass pane. At the corners, cut the spine of the gasket partway so it will bend around the corner. Continue fitting the gasket around the pane, cutting at the corners, until all four edges are covered. Trim off any excess gasket material.

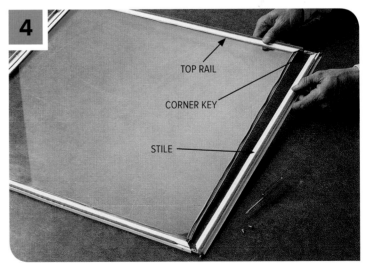

Slide the glass pane into the channels in the stiles and bottom rail of the sash frame. Insert corner keys into the top rail, then slip the other ends of the keys into the frame stiles. Press down on the top rail until the mitered corners are flush with the stiles. Drive the retaining screws back through the stiles and into the top rail to join the frame together. Reinsert the frame into the window.

How to Disassemble & Repair a Metal Sash Frame

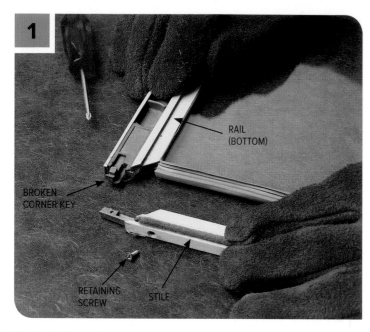

1

RAIL
(BOTTOM)

BROKEN
CORNER KEY

RETAINING
SCREW   STILE

2

CRIMP

BROKEN
CORNER KEY

SHOWN CUTAWAY
FOR CLARITY

Metal window sashes are held together at the corner joints by L-shaped pieces of hardware that fit into grooves in the sash frame pieces. To disassemble a broken joint, start by disconnecting the stile and rail at the broken joint—there is usually a retaining screw driven through the stile that must be removed.

Corner keys are secured in the rail slots with crimps that are punched into the metal over the key. To remove keys, drill through the metal in the crimped area using a drill bit the same diameter as the crimp. Carefully knock the broken key pieces from the frame slots with a screwdriver and hammer.

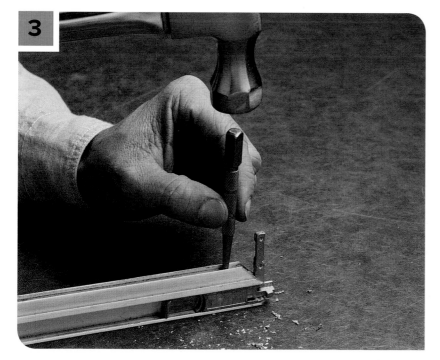

3

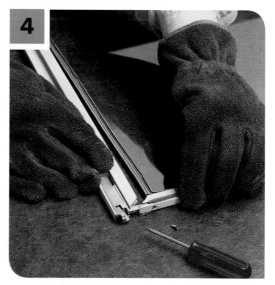

4

Insert the glass and gasket into the frame slots, then reassemble the frame and drive in retainer screws (for screen windows, replace the screening).

Locate matching replacement parts for the broken corner key, which is usually an assembly of two or three pieces. There are dozens of different types, so it is important that you save the old parts for reference. Most hardware stores carry a wide selection of common types. Insert the replacement corner key assembly into the slot in the rail. Use a nail set as a punch and rap it into the metal over the corner key, creating a new crimp to hold the key in place.

Tips for Maintaining Storm Windows & Doors

Lubricate the sliding assemblies on metal framed combination storm windows or doors once a year using penetrating lubricant.

Add a wind chain if your storm door does not have one. Wind chains prevent doors from blowing open too far, causing damage to the door hinges or closer. Set the chain so the door will not open more than 90°.

Adjust the door closer so it has the right amount of tension to close the door securely, without slamming. Most closers have tension-adjustment screws at the end of the cylinder farthest from the hinge side of the door.

TUNING UP GARAGE DOORS

O ver time, many good things become bad things, especially if they aren't well maintained. An overhead garage door is no exception. To keep everything running smoothly requires effort on three fronts: the door, the opener, and the opener's electronic safety sensors. Here's what you need to know to keep all three in tiptop shape.

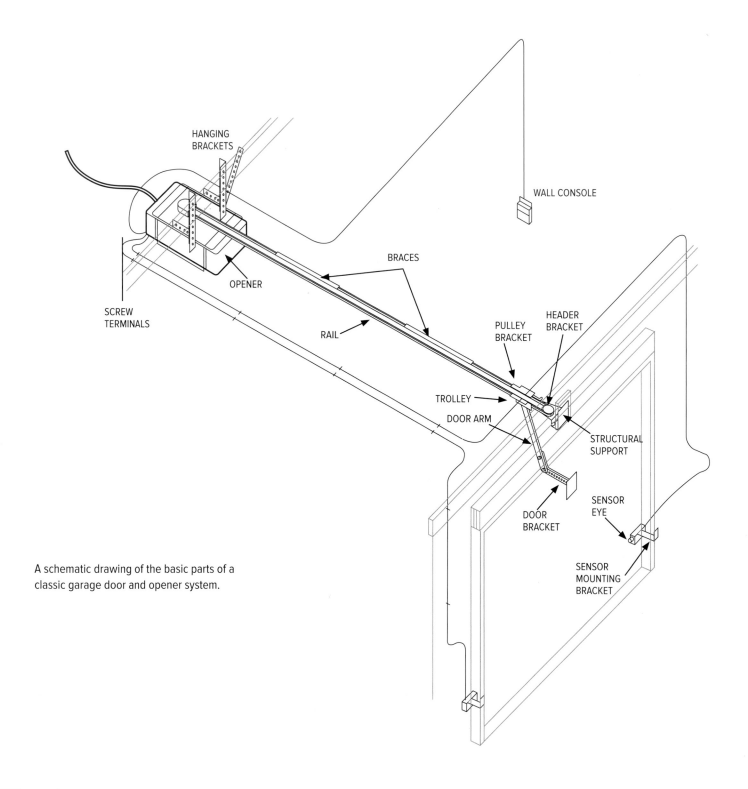

A schematic drawing of the basic parts of a classic garage door and opener system.

How to Tune Up a Garage Door

Begin the tune-up by lubricating the door tracks, pulleys, and rollers. Use a lightweight oil, not grease, for this job. The grease catches too much dust and dirt.

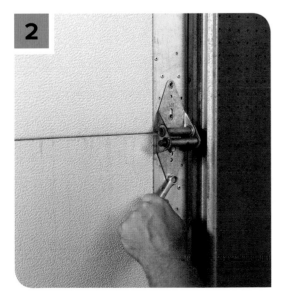

Remove clogged or damaged rollers from the door by loosening the nuts that hold the roller brackets. The roller will come with the bracket when the bracket is pulled free. Clean the rollers. Mineral spirits and kerosene are good solvents for cleaning roller bearings.

If the rollers are making a lot of noise as they move over the tracks, the tracks are probably out of alignment. To fix this, check the tracks for plumb. If they are out of plumb, the track mounting brackets must be adjusted.

HOW TO TUNE UP A GARAGE DOOR (continued)

4

To adjust out-of-plumb tracks, loosen all the track mounting brackets (usually 3 or 4 per track) and push the brackets into alignment. Once the track is plumb, tighten all the bolts.

5

Sometimes the door lock bar opens sluggishly because the return spring has lost its tension. The only way to fix this is to replace the spring. One end is attached to the body of the lock; the other end hooks onto the lock bar.

6

If a latch needs lubrication, use graphite in powder or liquid form. Don't use oil because it attracts dust that will clog the lock even more.

7

If the chain on your garage door opener is sagging more than ½" below the bottom rail, it can make a lot of noise and cause drive sprocket wear. Tighten the chain according to the directions in the owner's manual.

8

On openers with a chain, lubricate the entire length of the chain with penetrating oil. Do not use grease. Use the same lubricant if your opener has a drive screw instead.

9

Make sure that the sensors are "talking" to the opener properly. Start to close the door, then put your hand down between the two sensors. If the door stops immediately and reverses direction, it's working properly. If it's not, make the adjustment recommended in the owner's manual. If that doesn't do the trick, call a professional door installer and don't use the door until it passes this test.

"Repair" has a somewhat different connotation when it comes to home wiring than it does in other home systems. With walls, floors, insulations, roofing, and other systems, repair often means "patching." When you are dealing with your home electrical system, repair more often means replacing a failed device or connector with a safe and operational one. For example, if a light switch fails it would be a bad idea to try and identity and repair a fault in the switch. You are much better off (and code compliant) if you safely remove the failed switch and install a brand new one.

The electrical items that most frequently require actual repairs are light fixtures. If you include lamps and cords in this category, you've pretty much covered it. Some electrical failures result from poorly made connections in the original installation. Some, like switches and ceiling fans, will break down because they have moving parts and that always introduces stress.

When replacing part of an electrical fixture, the rule of thumb for finding the replacement part is to remove the broken part and bring it with you to a lighting or electrical supply store. Failing that, take down the make and serial number of the fixture so the clerk can look up part information for you.

Many home wiring repair and minor improvement projects are pretty simple and only dangerous if you are not careful and don't follow instructions and safety precautions. Some, such as replacing ordinary duplex receptacles with GFCI-protected devices will greatly improve the safety of your home.

Most basic home wiring repairs can be accomplished with relatively simple hand tools, such as screwdrivers, a utility knife, and pliers. As you take on more complex projects, you'll want to invest in some simple hand tools that are specific to home wiring. But in either case you will need some diagnostic tools to work safely, even on the simplest projects. The diagnostic tools above include, from left to right, a touchless circuit tester that lets you check for voltage without actually touching live wires or screw terminals; a plug-in tester for checking the polarity and grounding of a receptacle; and a multimeter, which is a crucial device for more complicated work but may not be needed for some of the more basic projects.

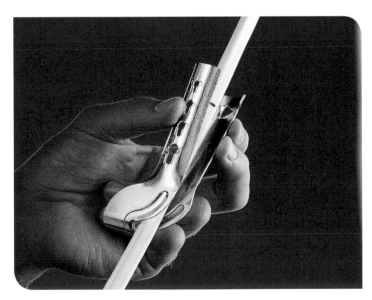

A cable ripper has one job only: to split the sheathing on wire cable (called NM cable) and expose the insulated wires inside without damaging them.

A wire stripper has graduated holes, like an old-style pencil sharpener, so you can select the opening that matches the gauge of the wire you are working with and use the tool to safely strip off the insulation without damaging the copper wire inside. You cannot make electrical connections with unstripped wire.

WIRING SAFETY

Safety should be the primary concern when working with anything having to do with electricity. Although most household electrical repairs and straightforward, always use caution and good judgment when working with electrical wiring or devices. Common sense and attentiveness prevent accidents.

The most basic rule when working with electricity is to **always shut off the power** to the area or device you are working on. This does not simply mean turn the switch controlling a device to "OFF." Switches can be defective and, depending on how that particular circuit is wired, there may be live current in the wires even if the device appears to be off. Someone also could inadvertently flip the switch on. Turn off power at the main circuit panel by shutting off circuit breakers or removing fuses. If you are working in an isolated area and know which circuit you may be coming in contact with, shutting off the breaker in only that circuit should be sufficient and allows you to retain power service elsewhere in the house. But always test the wiring and devices around the work area with a voltage tester or sensor to confirm that no power is present. And test thoroughly—it is always a possibility that power from multiple circuits is entering any electrical box. The absolute safest way to ensure you will not come in contact with electrical voltage is to shut off the main breakers in your panel, which cuts off all electrical service to the house. Even then, however, test for voltage.

OTHER IMPORTANT SAFETY CONSIDERATIONS WHEN WORKING WITH ELECTRICITY:

- Do not attempt any job unless you are certain how to do it and comfortable with the work. Never guess.
- Wear rubber-sole shoes when working with wiring—they are poor conductors of electricity in the event you get a shock.
- If you need to work on a ladder, use only wood or fiberglass ones—never metal.
- If you need to replace a circuit breaker or fuse, make certain that you buy one made by the same manufacturer as the electrical panel (they are not interchangeable) and that the new device is rated for the same amperage as the one you are replacing.

- Do not drill or saw into or otherwise penetrate any wall without either shutting off all power to the house first or testing with a voltage finder—this is a different tool than the voltage tester or sensor shown on page 70 and more closely resembles an electronic stud finder (some of which also have voltage finder capability).
- Never splice wires together unless the connection is made inside a certified junction box.
- Always use a wire connector of the correct size when splicing wires: a connector that is too big or too small can allow wires to fall out. Never make a splice using only electrical tape to bind the wires: that is not the purpose of electrical tape and is not allowed by codes.
- Do not attempt to remove cable sheathing or strip insulated conductors (wires) using a knife, scissors or any tool other than one rated for that purpose (see Cable ripper and Wire stripper, page 71).
- When attaching a wire to a screw terminal, make sure the required loop at the end of the wire is slightly larger than the diameter of the screw and orient the wire so the open end will be pressed further into a closed position when the screw is tightened in a clockwise direction.
- Test all connections by tugging lightly on them to make sure the wires are held fast and will not pull out or detach from a terminal from light pressure.
- Use the right tool for the job, and make sure the tool is clean and in good condition. In most home wiring projects, a very basic set of hand tools should include needle-nose pliers, linesman pliers (or wire cutters), phillips and slotted screwdrivers. Other tools will be required situationally.
- Never force wires or devices into a junction box. If you have the appropriate amount of cable extending into the box and do a neat job of arranging the connectors, any device you are mounting on the box should easily fit onto the box without pressure.
- Use only the regulation screws that are provided with your junction box to attach devices and faceplates to the box. A screw that it too long can extend too far into the box and contact the wires. One that is too narrow or wide or improperly threaded can slip out.
- Do not hesitate to contact a professional electrician when you encounter a situation that is outside of your knowledge and comfort level.

Locate and inspect your main service panel before starting any job. If your circuit map is up to date, try shutting off the power to the likely circuit you want to work on by flipping the switch on the appropriate breaker to OFF. Test the device you will be working on with a touchless circuit tester to make sure it is not receiving power. If there is any doubt in your mind, shut off the main circuit breakers at the top of the panel that provide power to all circuits.

Shut off power, and test the wires by placing a touchless voltage sensor within ½" of the wires. If the sensor beeps or lights up, then the circuit is still live and is not safe to work on. When the sensor does not beep or light up, the circuit is dead and may be worked upon. "Touchless" testers are safer than older neon circuit testers because you do not have to contact any potentially live wires.

BASIC WIRING SKILLS

Following are a few of the most elementary skills for working with electrical systems that are you may encounter when attempting the scope of repair projects featured in this book. Several of them you will not likely need, since the projects in this book are largely one-for-one replacements of devices and electrical fixtures and, therefore, do not require you to run new wiring. But because there are possible situations where you would need to work with new wires or cables (usually NM cable—which stands for nonmetallic), we are including some basic handling skills here. More complex projects will, of course, require more advanced skills that you will need to learn before attempting them.

How to Reset a Circuit Breaker

Open the door of the main service panel and locate the tripped breaker. It should be the only one flipped to an OFF position, and there is usually a red tab exposed.

To reset the breaker, first press the lever all the way to the OFF position, and then back to the ON position. If you were successful you should hear a clicking sound.

If an AFCI and GFCI breaker trips, press the "Push" button after you reset the breaker. If the breaker is functioning properly, it will trip to the OFF position. If it does not, the breaker likely is faulty and needs replacement.

How to Remove NM Cable Sheathing

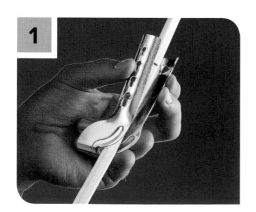

Feed the end of the cable into a cable ripper so the cutting point is 8" to 10" from the end and precisely centered side to side. Squeeze the tool to pierce the cable sheathing. Do not loosen your grip.

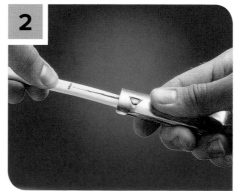

Holding the cable tightly, pull back on the cable ripper tool to create a longitudinal slice through the sheathing and insulating paper, all the way to the end.

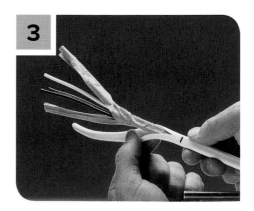

Pull down the sheathing and paper all the way to the initial point of the cut. Trim off the excess with scissors or the cutting jaws of a linesman pliers or a combination wire-stripper tool.

How to Strip Wire Insulation

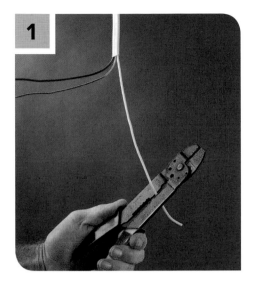

1

Cut the insulated conductors from your stripped cable (see previous page) so the wires extend 3" past the point where the sheathing resumes. You can use wire cutters or the cutting jaws on a combination wiring tool.

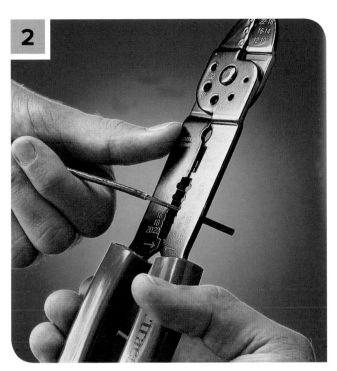

2

Insert each insulated conductor into the appropriately sized opening on your wire stripper or combination tool (in most homes this will be either 12 or 14-gauge). Clamp the jaws of the tool onto the insulation ¾" from the end. Rotate the tool back and forth slightly to pierce the sheathing all the way around, and then press the tool toward the end of the wire. The insulation should slide along the wire and drop off when you reach the end.

How to Connect Wires to Screw Terminals

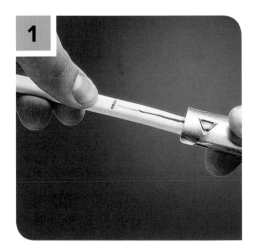

1

Strip ¾" of insulation from the wires in your cable (see previous page). With needle-nose pliers, bend a "C" shaped loop into the end of each wire. Avoid scratching the wire. The diameter of the C should be roughly ¼".

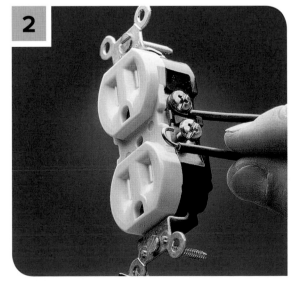

2

Unscrew the screw terminal on the device you are connecting to just enough to create clearance for the wire loops. Hook each wire loop over onto the shaft the correct screw terminal so the open end of the C is on the clockwise-turning side of the screw. Note that some devices have a slot in the casing next to the terminal for the wire to rest in. Make sure the feed side of the wire is in this slot to get the sturdiest connection. Use some tension to keep the loop in place as you tighten the screw so the screw head does not dislodge the loop. Tug lightly on the feed wire after you are done to make sure the connection is secure.

How to Join Wires with a Wire Connector

1

Ensure power is off and test for power. Grasp the wires to be joined in the jaws of a pair of linesman pliers. The ends of the wires should be flush and they should be parallel and touching. Rotate the pliers clockwise two or three turns to twist the wire ends together.

Twist a wire connector over the ends of the wires. Make sure the connector is the right size. Hand-twist the connector as far onto the wires as you can. There should be no bare wire exposed beneath the collar of the connector.

2

How to Pigtail Wires

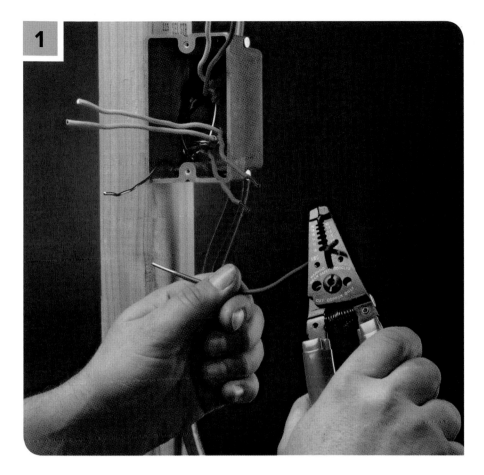

1

NOTE: Pigtailing is done mainly to avoid connecting multiple wires to one terminal, which is a code violation.

Cut a 6" length from a piece of insulated wire the same gauge and color as the wires it will be joining. Strip ¾" of insulation from each end of the insulated wire.

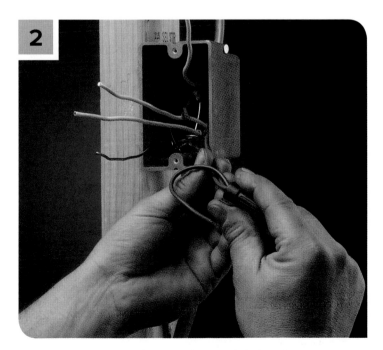

2

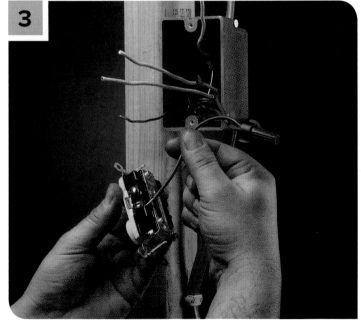

3

Join one end of the pigtail to the wires that will share the connection using a wire nut.

Connect the pigtail to the appropriate terminal on the receptacle or switch. Fold the wires neatly and press the fitting into the box.

REPLACING SWITCHES

Switches need replacement more than other electrical devices for a few reasons: They have moving parts and tend to wear out; They can have a prominent impact on your home décor and are often swapped out to change color or mechanic (lever versus rocker); New technical advances such as motion-activated switches, timed switches, or dimmer switches are more available and popular with homeowners.

Standard switches often confuse homeowners because they are unique in that they only have one wire connection (excepting the ground). The white neutral actually bypasses the switch and only the black power wire runs through it. The principle is simple: the power comes in through the switch. When the switch is open, power goes into the switch, passes through it, and comes out to an outgoing wire on the other side that leads to the switched device.

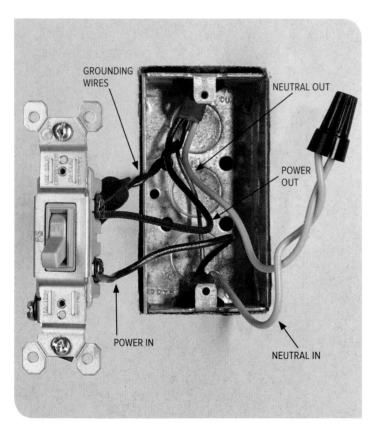

How a typical single-pole wall switch is wired depends on whether it is located in the middle of a circuit or at the end. It's a little complicated and has to do with whether or not there are multiple switches controlling a single fixture, usually a light. If the switch is in the middle, two 3-wire cables will be in the switch box: one from the power source and the other heading out to the load. If it is on the end, only one cable with three or four wires comes into the box.

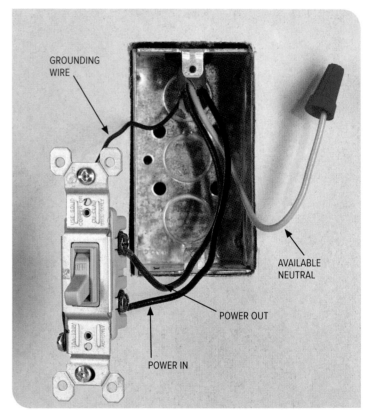

If you are making a one-for-one switch replacement, it is usually safe to assume that the old switch was wired correctly, and simply get a new switch that is configured like the old one and hook it up the same way.

How to Replace a Wall Switch

1

Turn off power to the switch at the main service panel. Remove the coverplate and the switch mounting screws. Withdraw the switch from the box, noting the locations of the wires and which terminals they are connected to.

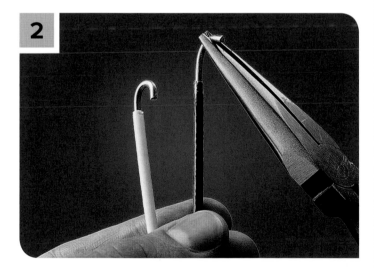

2

Disconnect the wires from the old switch. If the wires are not in pristine condition, strip off some insulation, cut ¼" to ½" of wire to create a clean end, and then rebend the terminal connection loops on the wires (see page 75). If the wires coming into the box were connected directly to the switch, reconnect them to the new switch in the same configuration. If the old wires were connected to the switch with pigtails (see previous page), create new pigtail wires and connect them to the new switch and to the incoming and outgoing wires in the same manner. Connect the grounding wire (usually bare copper) to the green grounding terminal on the switch. Fold the wire neatly behind the switch and insert the device back into the switch box. Fasten it to the box with the mounting screws and test. Reattach the coverplate.

Three-way Light Switches

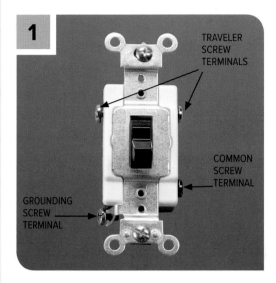

1

TRAVELER SCREW TERMINALS

COMMON SCREW TERMINAL

GROUNDING SCREW TERMINAL

Three-way switches are configured to enable two different switches to control a single fixture, usually a light. They are very common at the top and bottom of stairs. They are rather complicated, but if you need to replace a switch that looks like this, with three wire terminals (not including the grounding terminal), you can simply purchase a new three-way switch and hook it up the same way. Once you have the old switch out of the switch box, it's a good idea to tag the wire with tape the wire that is connected to the "Common" terminal on the old switch, since making sure this wire is connected to the "COM" terminal on the new one is the key to getting it right.

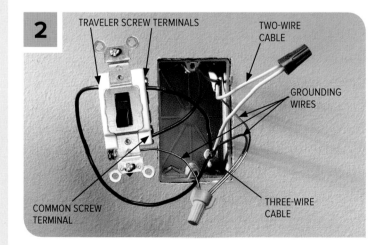

2

TRAVELER SCREW TERMINALS

TWO-WIRE CABLE

GROUNDING WIRES

COMMON SCREW TERMINAL

THREE-WIRE CABLE

The typical wiring scheme of a three-way switch. The key to getting the replacement right is to make sure the two traveler wires are connected to the two traveler terminal on the switch, and the common wire is connected to the common terminal on the new switch. The white neutrals should be connected with a wire connector but not attached to the switch. The ground wires should be pigtailed from the incoming cable and to the switch grounding terminal and then connected to the grounding screw on the switch box.

REPLACING RECEPTACLES

Receptacles (many call them plug-ins) are pretty reliable, but occasionally one will short-circuit or the electrical contacts will separate, causing failure. Your home may have old two-slot receptacles that you'd like to upgrade to three-prong types with a ground to accept a three-prong plug (not as simple as swapping out with a new device). You may wish to bring your kitchen or bathroom up to code by replacing a standard receptacle with one that has built-in Ground-fault Current Interrupter protection (this is a simple one-for-one replacement). You may even want to replace your plug-in simply to update the look of your walls, although you will not find as wide a selection of designer receptacles, like you will for switches.

The main considerations when replacing a receptacle are:
• SAFETY Be sure the circuit power is shut off and test thoroughly with a touchless voltage sensor (see page 73).
• Make sure the replacement device has the same amperage rating (usually 15 or 20 amps) as the one you are replacing
• Make sure the wires that are attached to the new receptacle are in solid condition and the wire connections (be they screw terminals or push-in) are very secure.
• The new receptacle should be securely mounted to the box with the correct mounting screws.
• The coverplate should fully conceal the wall opening containing the receptacle box, with no gaps anywhere.

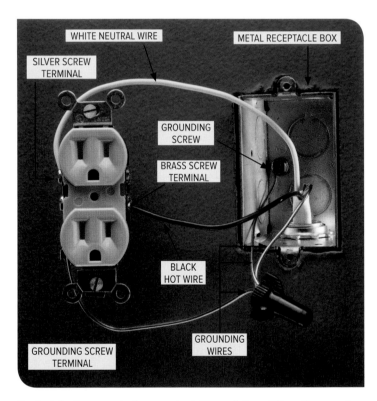
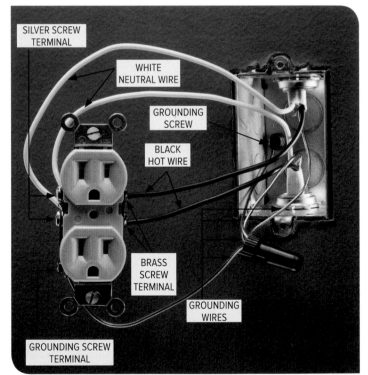

Typical duplex receptacles are wired, like switches, differently according to whether they are located in the middle or end of a circuit. Also like switches, it is good to understand the difference if you are replacing a receptacle, but in most cases simply hooking up the new device in the same manner will give you good results. But always check your installation with a plug-in tester (see page 82) to make sure it is functioning properly. The left photo above represents an end-of-run installation where no additional receptacles or devices follow the receptacle in the circuit. In this case, only one cable enters the box and two of the screw terminals are unused. In the right photo, both an incoming cable and an outgoing cable are present, and all four terminal are connected.

Types of Receptacles

15-amp, 120-volt two-slot receptacles have not been installed with any frequency for over 50 years. The later ones have one tall slot and one short slot to accommodate polarized plugs. If you have these in your house, you probably have a drawer full of three-prong plug-in adapters as well. For ease of use, these may be replaced with three-slot receptacles, but test the new receptacle with a plug-in tester to see if it is grounded. If not, the receptacle box or the house wiring are not properly grounded, in which case you should consult an electrician.

15-amp, 120-volt three-slot receptacles are standard in 15-amp home circuits. See "Up or Down" below. The device shown here is also tamper-resistant in that the slots are protected so children can't poke small items into them. Tamper-resistant receptacles are required in new construction.

20-amp, 120-volt receptacles are designed for 20-amp circuits, required in kitchens, among other places. The T-shaped slot identifies them as 20-amp and accommodates the plugs on some appliances and tools that draw high amperage and, therefore, have a corresponding T-shaped plug.

15-amp, 240-volt receptacles have two horizontal slots and are installed on a 240-volt circuit. They are used most often for window air conditioners. Other 240-volt receptacles, installed mostly on dedicated clothes dryer or electric water heater or oven circuits, carry higher amperage (30 or 50 amps on most cases) also have unique slot configurations. Because of their high amperage, it is best to have them serviced by a professional electrician if they develop issues.

UP OR DOWN?

At some point, you have probably seen a receptacle that is installed with the D-shaped hole for the grounding pin on the plug facing up. This was not an error by the installer. In fact, the orientation of the grounding slot is a much-debated subject, even among professional electricians. While we are accustomed to seeing receptacles with the grounding slot at the bottom, some argue that this poses a safety risk. If a plug is not fully inserted into the receptacle, but is far enough in to be drawing power, any item that might happen to slide along the wall could make contact with the live plug prongs, causing a short circuit and potentially a fire or electrical shock. By installing the receptacle with the D-shaped grounding slot at the top, a wayward item might still make contact but because the grounding prong on a plug does not carry current it will not result in a short circuit. National electrical codes do not endorse either orientation, but many electricians prefer ground-slot up installations.

Tips for Working with Receptacles

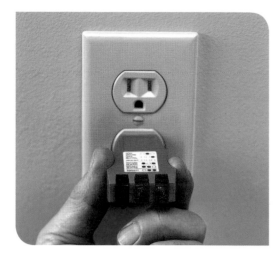

A plug-in tester is a very important and very easy-to-use wiring diagnostic tool. The tool contains three lights and if the receptacle is improperly connected it will display various illumination patterns most have an on-board key. They will identify if the receptacle is not properly grounded or if a continuity problem exists, but there are other possible miswiring issues it cannot detect that can be diagnosed only with a multimeter.

A multimeter (also called an ammeter) is a more advanced wiring-diagnostic tool that can perform multiple diagnostic functions depending on the settings. They are very useful tools to have if you wish to advance your home wiring skills. Using one correctly takes some studying, so read the manual carefully if you buy one.

GFCI receptacles provide point-of-service ground fault protection and are required in any area of the home where moisture is present, including kitchens, bathrooms, basement, and garages. They are rated for either 15- or 20-amp circuits, so make sure the one you buy matches the amperage of the circuit it is being installed in (see previous page). You can also provide ground fault protection to an entire circuit by installing a GFCI circuit breaker in your main panel. See pages 86–87.

Common Mistakes Made Wiring Receptacles

Mistake: Bare wires extend past a screw terminal. Exposed wires can cause a short circuit if they come in contact with a metal receptacle box or other wires inside the box. Here, there is too much exposed wire on both the infeed and outfeed side of the terminal.

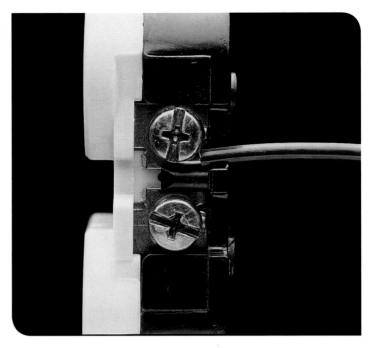

Correct: Wire insulation touches the screw terminal and the loose end of the wire is tucked neatly underneath the terminal screwhead.

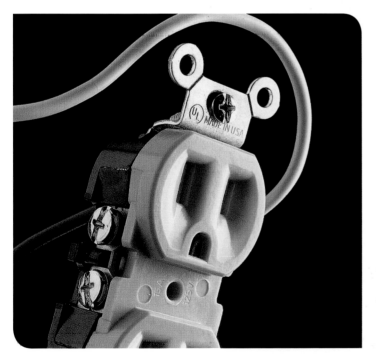

Mistake: Wires are connected to the wrong terminals. Receptacles have brass and silver terminals: brass is for the live wires (usually black) and silver is for the white neutral wires. Although a receptacle wired in this manner may appear to function normally, in fact it will deliver power to the long neutral slot of the receptacle, so power will be traveling to the load through the neutral path.

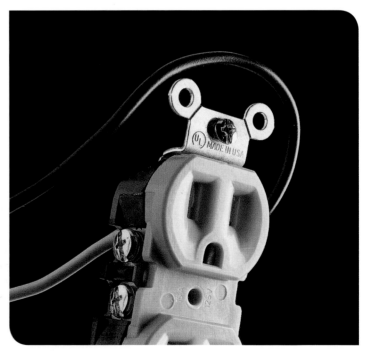

Correct: In a correct installation, all live power-carrying wires are connected to brass terminals on the receptacle, and all white neutral wire are connected to silver terminals.

NOTE: One of the limitations of plug-in testers (previous page) is that most will not detect if current is flowing to the neutral slot. You'll need to either test with a multimeter or make a visual inspection of the terminal connections.

GFCI RECEPTACLES

If you are building a new house or doing a major remodeling project, it is required that all circuits in potentially wet areas have ground fault interruption protection. But even if your home is not undergoing remodeling, replacing standard receptacles with GFCI receptacles is a very prudent idea because it means you will have a safer home.

GFCI receptacles are basically sensors that detect changes in current flow and instantly shut off power to any device on the protected circuit. This is important because the current usually are caused by faults in the appliances that are plugged into the circuit. Faults can be caused by an electrical malfunction or short circuit in the appliance (possibly caused by exposure to moisture), which can easily lead to a fire.

If you replace an ordinary receptacle with a GFCI receptacle, everything you plug into that outlet will be protected, but the entire circuit will not be. You can solve this by replacing all of the receptacles on the circuit with a GFCI receptacle. You can also wire one GFCI in a series fashion so it protects all outlets down-line from it. This is efficient, and also a relatively tricky wiring job unless you have a lot of wiring experience. It also increasing the likelihood of nuisance tripping of the one GFCI, which can happen when you get an occasional (and not dangerous) small drop in current flow. The best protection is to replace the breaker for that circuit in your main service panel with a GFCI breaker. This, too, is not a job for a begging home electrician.

NOTE: The sequence on the next page shows how to replace a standard receptacle with a GFCI. If you are simply making a one-for-one replacement of a standard receptacle, the steps are the same.

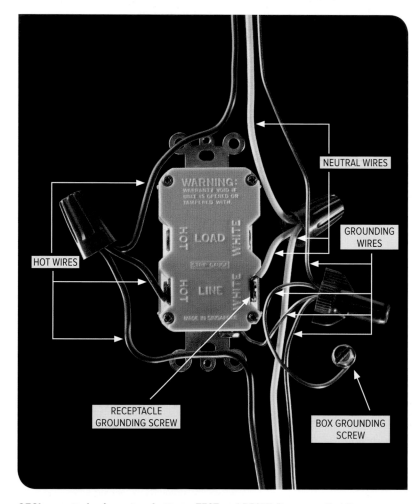

GFCI receptacles have two buttons: TEST and RESET. To ensure that they are functioning, press the TEST button manufacturers suggest you test at least once a year. This should cause the outlet to lose power immediately. Then push the RESET button to restore power. If the GFCI trips from an occasional nuisance change in current level, hit the RESET button. If the GFCI trips again, it likely means that one of the appliances plugged into that outlet has a fault.

How to Install a GFCI for Single-Location Protection

1

Shut off power to the circuit at the main circuit breaker and test with a voltage sensor. Remove the coverplate and the mounting screws holding the receptacle to the box. Without touching the screw terminals or wires, withdraw the receptacle from the box. Test again to confirm it is not getting power.

2

Disconnect the white neutral wires from the old receptacle first. Create a white wire pigtail if none is present in the box (see page 77). Join all white wires in the box, plus the pigtail, with an appropriate wire connector (see page 76).

3

Connect the free end of the white pigtail wire to the silver terminal marked LINE on the GFCI receptacle.

NOTE: The installation shown here is for single-location protection. Your GFCI receptacle will have a second set of brass and silver terminals marked "LOAD." These are for use if you are wiring the device to feed additional circuits downstream. For the project shown here do not attach any wires to the LINE terminals.

4

Disconnect all black wires from the old receptacle. Create a black pigtail if none is present. Connect all black wires in the box, plus the pigtail, with an appropriate wire connector. Attach the free end of the pigtail to the brass terminal marked LINE on the GFCI receptacle.

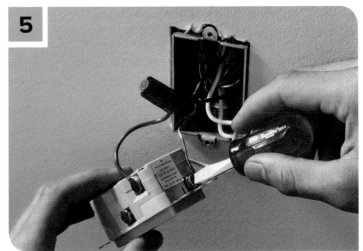

5

If a grounding wire is available, connect it to the green grounding screw on the GFCI. Neatly fold the wires behind the GFCI and insert it into the receptacle box. Because GFCI receptacles have slightly larger bodies than standard receptacles, the fit is likely to be more snug than it was with the old unit. Do not force the GFCI in. If the box is overcrowded, it will need to be replaced with a larger box. Mount the GFCI to box with the provided mounting screws and attach the coverplate (usually provided with the GFCI).

REPAIRING LIGHT FIXTURES

Light fixtures are attached permanently to ceilings or walls. They include wall-hung sconces, ceiling-hung globe fixtures, recessed light fixtures, and chandeliers. Most light fixtures are easy to repair using basic tools and inexpensive parts.

If a light fixture fails, always make sure the lightbulb is screwed in tightly and is not burned out. A faulty lightbulb is the most common cause of light fixture failure. If the light fixture is controlled by a wall switch, also check the switch as a possible source of problems.

Light fixtures can fail because the sockets or built-in switches wear out. Some fixtures have sockets and switches that can be removed for minor repairs. These parts are held to the base of the fixture with mounting screws or clips. Other fixtures have sockets and switches that are joined permanently to the base. If this type of fixture fails, purchase and install a new light fixture.

Damage to light fixtures can occur because homeowners install lightbulbs with wattage ratings that are too high. Prevent overheating and light fixture failures by using lightbulbs that only match the wattage ratings printed on the fixtures.

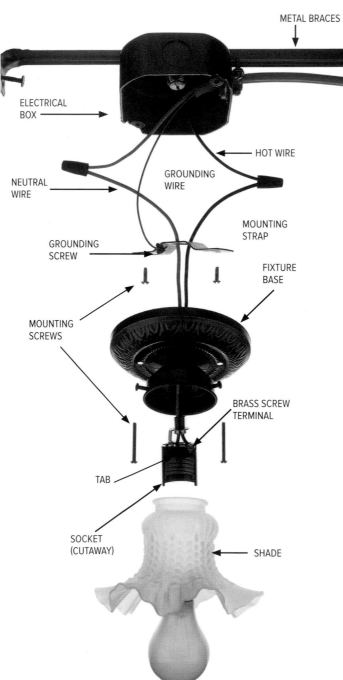

METAL BRACES

ELECTRICAL BOX

HOT WIRE

GROUNDING WIRE

NEUTRAL WIRE

MOUNTING STRAP

GROUNDING SCREW

FIXTURE BASE

MOUNTING SCREWS

BRASS SCREW TERMINAL

TAB

SOCKET (CUTAWAY)

SHADE

In a typical light fixture, a black hot wire is connected to a brass screw terminal on the socket. Power flows to a small tab at the bottom of the metal socket and through a metal filament inside an incandescent bulb. The power heats the filament and causes it to glow. If you are using compact fluorescent bulbs, the electricity flowing through the socket excites the gases inside the bulb causing them to give off light. In the case of LED bulbs, the power is sent to microchips that redirect it to light emitting diodes. In all cases, the current then flows back through the threaded portion of the socket and through the white neutral wire back to the main service panel.

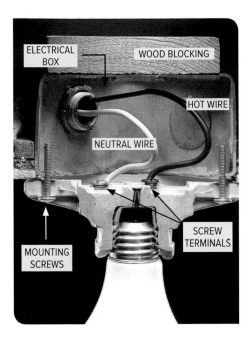

ELECTRICAL BOX

WOOD BLOCKING

HOT WIRE

NEUTRAL WIRE

MOUNTING SCREWS

SCREW TERMINALS

Before 1959, light fixtures often were mounted directly to an electrical box or to plaster lath. Electrical codes now require that fixtures be attached to mounting straps that are anchored to the electrical boxes. If you have a light fixture attached to plaster lath, install an approved electrical box with a mounting strap to support the fixture.

TROUBLESHOOTING LIGHT FIXTURES

PROBLEM	REPAIR
Wall- or ceiling-mounted fixture flickers or does not light.	1. Check for faulty lightbulb. 2. Check wall switch and replace, if needed. 3. Check for loose wire connections in electrical box. 4. Test socket and replace, if needed. 5. Replace light fixture.
Built-in switch on fixture does not work.	1. Check for faulty lightbulb. 2. Check for loose wire connections on switch. 3. Replace switch. 4. Replace light fixture.
Chandelier flickers or does not light.	1. Check for faulty lightbulb. 2. Check wall switch and replace, if needed. 3. Check for loose wire connections in electrical box. 4. Test sockets and fixture wires, and replace, if needed.
Recessed fixture flickers or does not light.	1. Check for faulty lightbulb. 2. Check wall switch, and replace, if needed. 3. Check for loose wire connections in electrical box. 4. Test fixture, and replace, if needed. 5. Wait a few minutes. If light activates, fixture is overheating. Remove insulation from around fixture.

How to Remove a Light Fixture & Test a Socket

1

Turn off the power to the light fixture at the main panel. Remove the lightbulb and any shade or globe, then remove the mounting screws holding the fixture base and the electrical box or mounting strap. Carefully pull the fixture base away from the box. Test for power with a circuit tester.

2

Disconnect the light fixture base by loosening the screw terminals. If the fixture has wire leads instead of screw terminals, remove the light fixture base by unscrewing the wire connectors.

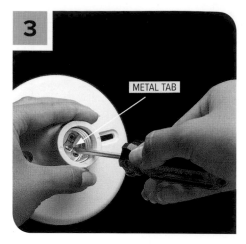

3

METAL TAB

Adjust the metal tab at the bottom of the fixture socket by prying it up slightly with a small screwdriver. This adjustment will improve the contact between the socket and the lightbulb.

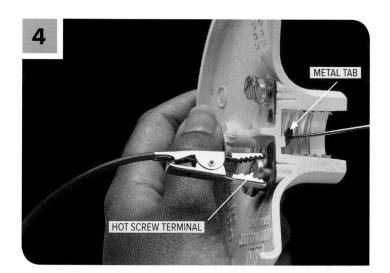

4

METAL TAB

HOT SCREW TERMINAL

Test the socket (shown cutaway) by attaching the clip of a multimeter (see page 82) to the hot screw terminal (or black wire lead) and touching the probe of the tester to the metal tab in the bottom of the socket. The multimeter should indicate continuity. If not, the socket is faulty and must be replaced.

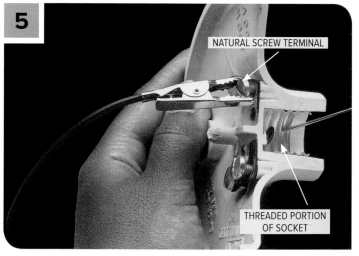

5

NATURAL SCREW TERMINAL

THREADED PORTION OF SOCKET

Attach the multimeter clip to the neutral screw terminal (or white wire lead), and touch the probe to the threaded portion of the socket. The multimeter should indicate continuity. If not, the socket is faulty and must be replaced. If the socket is permanently attached, replace the fixture.

How to Replace a Socket

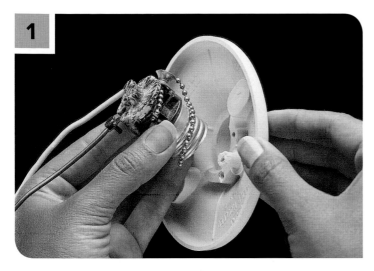

1

Remove the old light fixture. Remove the socket from the fixture. The socket may be held by a screw, clip, or retaining ring. Disconnect wires attached to the socket.

2

Purchase an identical replacement socket. Connect the white wire to the silver screw terminal on the socket, and connect the black wire to the brass screw terminal. Attach the socket to the fixture base, and reinstall the fixture.

How to Test & Replace a Built-in Light Switch

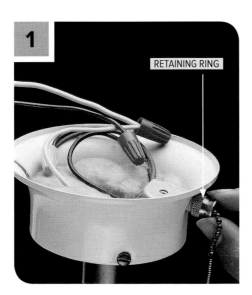

1

RETAINING RING

Remove the light fixture. Unscrew the retaining ring holding the switch.

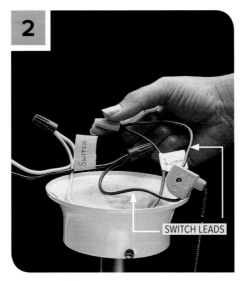

2

SWITCH LEADS

Label the wires connected to the switch leads. Disconnect the switch leads, and remove the switch.

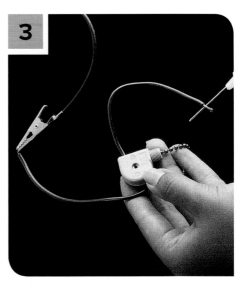

3

Test the switch by attaching the clip of a multi-meter to one of the switch leads and holding the probe to the other lead. Operate the switch control. If the switch is good, the multimeter will indicate continuity when the switch is in one position but not both. If the switch is faulty, purchase and install a duplicate switch. Remount the light fixture, and turn on the power at the main service panel.

REPAIRING CHANDELIERS

epairing a chandelier requires special care. Because chandeliers are heavy, it is a good idea to work with a helper when removing a chandelier. Support the fixture to prevent its weight from pulling against the wires.

Chandeliers have two fixture wires that are threaded through the support chain from the electrical box to the hollow base of the chandelier. The socket wires connect to the fixture wires inside this base.

Fixture wires are identified as hot and neutral. Look closely for a raised stripe on one of the wires. This is the neutral wire that is connected to the white circuit wire and white socket wire. The other smooth fixture wire is hot and is connected to the black wires.

If you have a newer chandelier, it may have a grounding wire that runs through the support chain to the electrical box. If this wire is present, make sure it is connected to the grounding wires in the electrical box

How to Repair a Chandelier

Label any lights that are not working using masking tape. Turn off power to the fixture at the panel. Remove lightbulbs and all shades or globes.

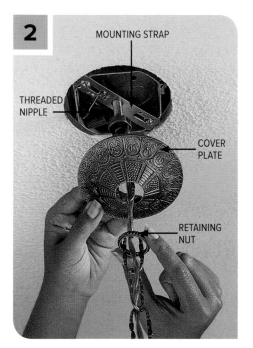

Turn off power at the main panel. Unscrew the retaining nut, and lower the decorative coverplate away from the electrical box. Most chandeliers are supported by a threaded nipple attached to a mounting strap.

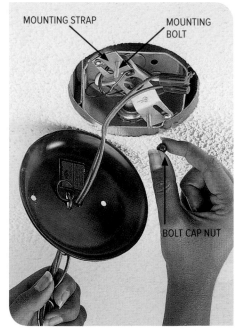

MOUNTING VARIATION: Some chandeliers are supported only by the coverplate that is bolted to the electrical box mounting strap. These types do not have a threaded nipple.

3

GROUNDING SCREW

THREADED NIPPLE

Test for power with a circuit tester. Disconnect fixture wires by removing the wire connectors. Unscrew the threaded nipple and carefully place the chandelier on a flat surface.

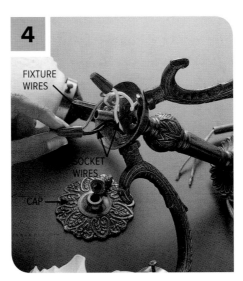

4

FIXTURE WIRES

SOCKET WIRES

CAP

Remove the cap from the bottom of the chandelier, exposing the wire connections inside the hollow base. Disconnect the socket wires and fixture wires.

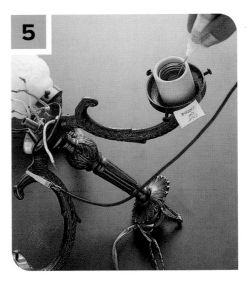

5

Test the socket by attaching the clip of the multimeter to the black socket wire and touching the probe to the tab in the socket. Repeat with the socket threads and the white socket wire. If the multimeter does not indicate continuity, the socket must be replaced.

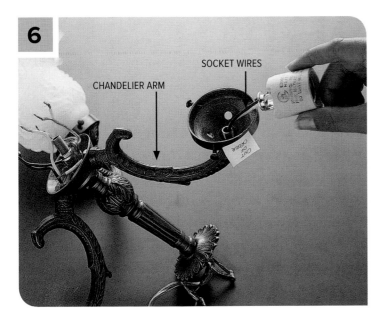

6

CHANDELIER ARM

SOCKET WIRES

Remove a faulty socket by loosening any mounting screws or clips and pulling the socket and socket wires out of the fixture arm. Purchase and install a new chandelier socket, threading the socket wires through the fixture arm.

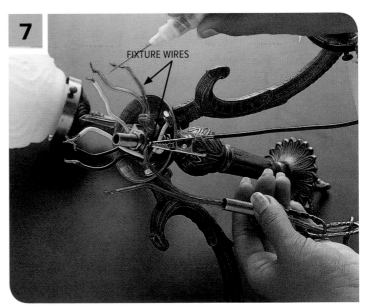

7

FIXTURE WIRES

Test each fixture wire by attaching the clip of the multimeter to one end of the wire and touching the probe to other end. If there is no continuity, the wire must be replaced. Install new wires, if needed, then reassemble and rehang the chandelier.

FLUORESCENT LIGHTS

With the advent of compact fluorescents and LED options, the traditional fluorescent fixture, with its long tubular lamps and rectangular metal housing, or troffer, has been relegated mostly to garages, workshops and basements these days. Nevertheless, you can still find fluorescent fixtures in just about every home, and they do require attention from time to time.

Fluorescent lights are relatively trouble free and use less energy than incandescent lights. A typical fluorescent lamp lasts about three years and produces two to four times as much light per watt as a standard incandescent lightbulb. The most frequent problem with a fluorescent light fixture is a failed lamp (tube). If a fluorescent light fixture begins to flicker or does not light fully, remove and examine the lamp.

Fluorescent light fixtures also can malfunction if the sockets are cracked or worn. Inexpensive replacement sockets are available at any hardware store and can be installed in a few minutes. If a fixture does not work, even after the tube and sockets have been serviced, the ballast probably is defective. Faulty ballasts often give themselves away by making a humming sound.

Fluorescent light fixtures usually contain a small cylindrical or button-shaped device, called a starter, located near one of the sockets. When a tube begins to flicker, replace both the tube and the starter. Turn off the power, and remove the starter by pushing it slightly and turning it counterclockwise. Install a replacement that matches the old starter.

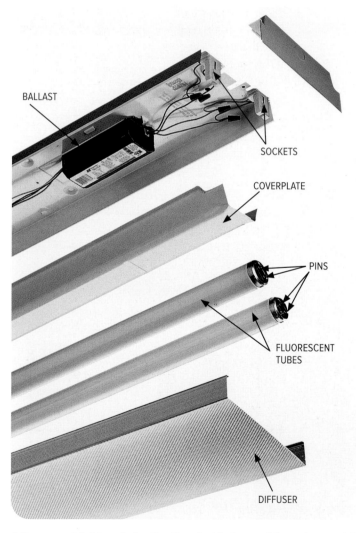

A fluorescent light works by directing electrical current through a special gas-filled tube that glows when energized. A translucent diffuser protects the fluorescent tube and softens the light. A coverplate protects a special transformer, called a ballast. The ballast regulates the flow of 120-volt household current to the sockets. The sockets transfer power to metal pins that extend into the tube.

SAFETY TIP
Never dispose of old tubes by breaking them. Fluorescent tubes contain a small amount of hazardous mercury. Check with your local environmental control agency or health department for disposal guidelines.

FLOURESCENT LAMPS

The "bulb" in a fluorescent light fixture is technically called a "lamp." Replacing a failed one is a bit trickier than screwing in a new lightbulb, and so is selecting the correct replacement lamp.

The surest way to obtain the correct fluorescent lamp is simply to bring the old lamp to the store with you and find an identical one. Most hardware stores will dispose of your old lamp for you, although some may tack on a small environmental charge for the service. Or, you can find the lamp type printed near its end. The type information starts with the letter "T,"

If you are unsure if the lamp is burned out, make a visual inspection. The top lamp is fine and shows no blackening; the middle lamp is headed to failure and may flicker—replace it; the bottom lamp is burned out. If you have a multimeter, you can perform a continuity test on the lamp to assess its condition.

which stands for "tube," as in "T12." The one-or-two-digit numeral following the T indicates the diameter in eighth-inches. So a T12 (the most common size) is $^{12}/_8$" in dia., or 1½". The T rating is usually preceded by an "F" and a numeral, which is the length of the lamp in inches. So a 40" lamp would be "F40." Length measurements include the pins. If you match the F and T ratings, the lamp should fit.

Light color

You'll find a number of color choices, which is really a reference to the temperature of the light. In most hardware stores and building centers, you'll see:

- "Warm" or "Warm white," which is the closest approximation to the light temperature of an incandescent bulb.
- "Cool white" or "Bright white," which actually has a hotter temperature than warm and is good for low-light areas like basements and garages.
- "Daylight" or "Full spectrum," which is meant to approximate natural light and is generally easy on the eyes.

The best advice on light color is to avoid mixing them in the same room. And make sure your new lamp has the same wattage rating as the old one.

How to Remove/Replace a Fluorescent Lamp

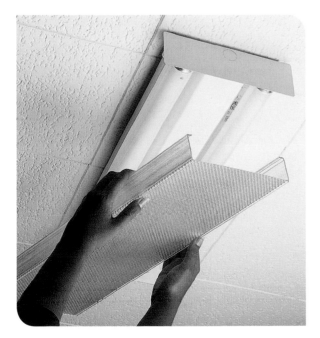

Turn off power to the light fixture at the switch. Remove the diffuser—be careful, these can be fragile. Most often you need to press inward slightly on the sides of the diffuser to release it.

Remove the fluorescent lamp by rotating it ¼ turn in either direction and sliding the tube out of both sockets at the same time. Do not force it. To install a new lamp, align the pins on each end with the slot in each socket, insert the lamp into the sockets, and then twist it ¼ turn in either direction until it is locked securely (inset photo). Reattach the diffuser and turn on the power at the switch.

How to Replace a Fluorescent Socket

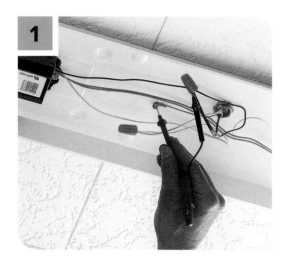

Turn off the power at the main electrical service panel, not simply at the switch. Remove the diffuser and fluorescent lamp (see previous page). Remove the coverplate protecting the ballast and fixture wiring. Test for power by touching one probe of an electrical circuit tester to the grounding screw and inserting the other probe into the hot wire connector.

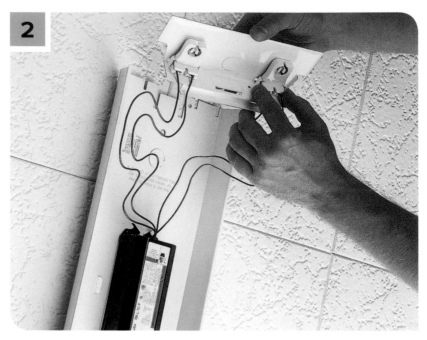

Detach the faulty socket from the fixture housing. Some sockets slide out, while others must be unscrewed.

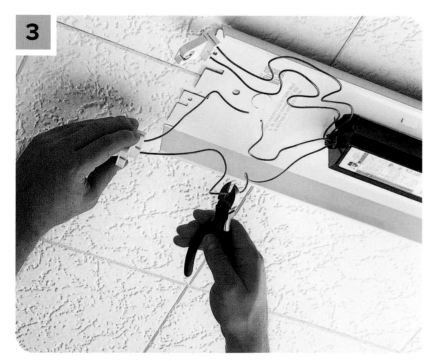

Disconnect the wires attaching the socket to the ballast. For sockets with push-in fittings, remove the wires by inserting a small screwdriver into the release openings. If your socket has screw terminal connections, loosen the screw and detach the wires. If your socket has lead wires that are fixed within the socket (as seen above), the wires must be cut.

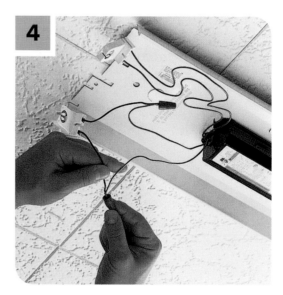

Bring the socket to the hardware store and use it as a guide to find the correct replacement. Connect the socket wires to the ballast wires by making the push-in or screw terminal connections at the socket, or by joining the ballast and socket wires with a wire connector if your socket has preattached wires (as seen above). Replace the coverplate and then the fluorescent lamp and diffuser. Restore power to the fixture at the panel and test.

How to Replace a Fluorescent Ballast

1

Turn off electrical power at the main service panel. Remove the diffuser, fluorescent lamp, and coverplate, and then test for power using an electrical circuit tester (see page 88). With the wires from the ballast disconnected, detach the ballast from the fixture housing by removing the attachment screws with a ratchet wrench or screwdriver. Support the ballast so it does not fall.

2

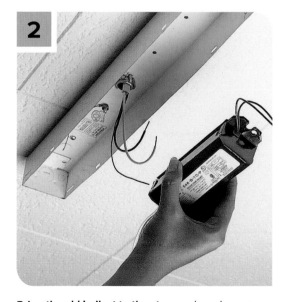

Bring the old ballast to the store and purchase a replacement ballast with the same wattage rating and physical configuration. Secure the new ballast to the fixture housing with the mounting screws.

3

Attach the ballast wires to the socket wires using wire connectors, screw terminal connections, or push-in fittings (see previous page). Reinstall the coverplate, and fluorescent lamp. Turn on power to the light fixture at the panel and test. Reattach the diffuser.

REPAIRING & ADJUSTING CEILING FANS

Ceiling fans contain rapidly moving parts, making them more susceptible to trouble than many other electrical fixtures. Installation is a relatively simple matter, but repairing a ceiling fan can be very frustrating. The most common problems you'll encounter are balance and noise issues and switch failure, usually precipitated by the pull chain breaking. In most cases, both problems can be corrected without removing the fan from the ceiling. But if you have difficulty on ladders or simply don't care to work overhead, consider removing the fan when replacing the switch.

Ceiling fans are subject to a great deal of vibration and stress, so it's not uncommon for switches and motors to fail. Minimize wear and tear by making sure blades are in balance so the fan doesn't wobble.

How to Troubleshoot Blade Wobble

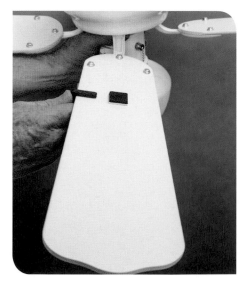

Start by checking and tightening all hardware used to attach the blades to the mounting arms and the mounting arms to the motor. Hardware tends to loosen over time, and this is frequently the cause of wobble.

If wobble persists, try switching around two of the blades. Often this is all it takes to get the fan back into balance. If a blade is damaged or warped, replace it.

OPTION: Fan blade wobble also may be corrected using small weights that are affixed to the tops of the blades. For an easy DIY fix, you can use electrical tape and washer and some trial and error. You can also purchase fan blade weight kits for a couple of dollars. These kits include clips for marking the position of the weights as you relocate them as well as self-adhesive weights that can be stuck to the blade once you have found the sweet spot.

How to Fix a Loose Wire Connection

A leading cause of fan failure is loose wire connections. To inspect these connections, first shut off the power to the fan. Remove the fan blades to gain access, and then remove the canopy that covers the ceiling box and fan mounting bracket. Most canopies are secured with screws on the outside shell. Have a helper hold the fan body while you remove the screws so it won't fall.

Once the canopy is removed, you'll see black, white, green, copper, and possibly blue wires. Hold a voltage sensor within ½" of these wires with the wall switch that controls the fan in the ON position. The black and blue wires should cause the sensor to beep if power is present.

Shut off power and test the wires by placing a voltage sensor within ½" of the wires. If the sensor beeps or lights up, then the circuit is still live and is not safe to work on. When the sensor does not beep or light up, the circuit is dead and may be worked upon.

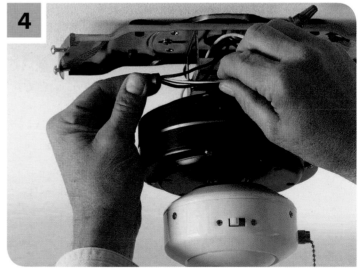

When you have confirmed that there is no power, check all the wire connections to make certain each is tight and making good contact. You may be able to see that a connection has come apart and needs to be remade. But even if you see one bad connection, check them all by gently tugging on the wire connectors. If the wires pull out of the wire connector or the connection feels loose, unscrew the wire connector from the wires. Turn the power back on and see if the problem has been solved.

How to Replace a Ceiling Fan Pull-Chain Switch

Turn off the power at the panel. Use a screwdriver to remove the three to four screws that secure the bottom cap on the fan switch housing. Lower the cap to expose the wires that supply power to the pull-chain switch.

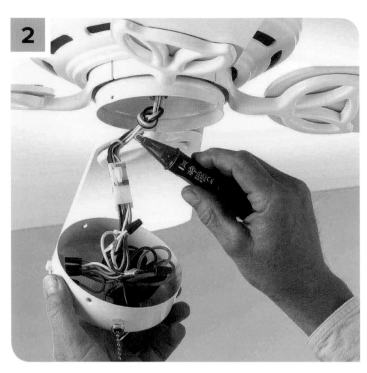

Test the wires by placing a voltage sensor within ½" of the wires. If the sensor beeps or lights up, then the circuit is still live and is not safe to work on. When the sensor does not beep or light up, the circuit is dead and may be worked upon.

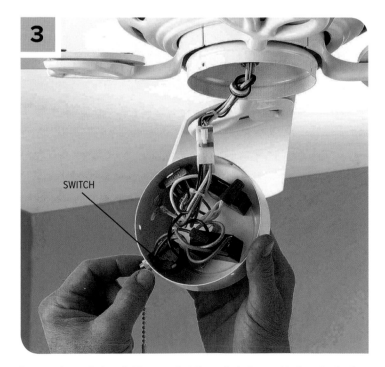

Locate the switch unit (the part that the pull chain used to be attached to if it broke off); it's probably made of plastic. You'll need to replace the whole switch. Fan switches are connected with three to eight wires, depending on the number of speed settings.

Attach a small piece of tape to each wire that enters the switch and write an identifying number on the tape. Start at one side of the switch and label the wires in the order they're attached.

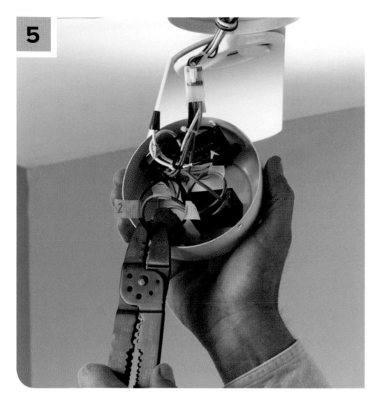

5

Disconnect the old switch wires, in most cases by cutting the wires off as close to the old switch as possible.

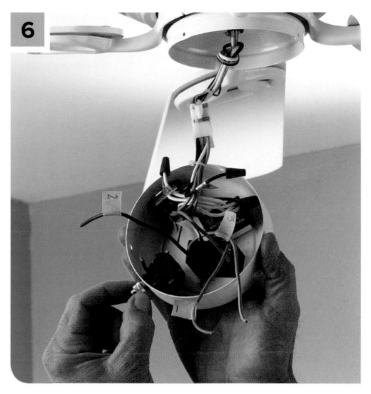

6

Remove the switch. Unscrew the retaining nut that secures the switch to the switch housing. There may be one or two screws that hold it in place or it may be secured to the outside of the fan with a small knurled nut, which you can loosen with needle-nose pliers. Purchase an identical new switch.

7

Connect the new switch using the same wiring configuration as on the old model. To make connections, first use a wire stripper to strip ¾" of insulation from the ends of each of the wires coming from the fan motor (the ones you cut in step 5). Attach the wires to the new switch in the same order and configuration as they were attached to the old switch. Secure the new switch in the housing, and make sure all wires are tucked neatly inside. Reattach the bottom cap. Restore power to the fan. Test all the fan's speeds to make sure all the connections are good.

REPLACING PLUGS & CORDS

Replace an electrical plug whenever you notice bent or loose prongs, a cracked or damaged casing, or a missing insulating faceplate. A damaged plug poses a shock and fire hazard. Replacement plugs are available in different styles to match common appliance cords. Always choose a replacement that is similar to the original plug. Flat-cord and quick-connect plugs are used with light-duty appliances, such as lamps and radios. Round-cord plugs are used with larger appliances, including those that have three-prong grounding plugs.

Some tools and appliances use polarized plugs. A polarized plug has one wide prong and one narrow prong, corresponding to the neutral and hot slots found in a standard receptacle.

If there is room in the plug body, tie the individual wires in an underwriter's knot to secure the plug to the cord (see photo, opposite page, top).

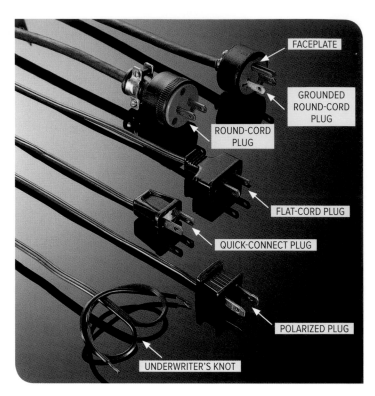

Common replaceable plug types

How to Install a Quick-Connect Plug

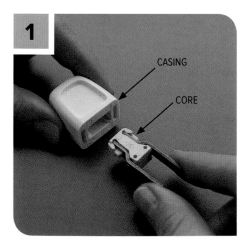

Squeeze the prongs of the new quick-connect plug together slightly and pull the plug core from the casing. Cut the old plug from the flat-cord wire with a combination tool, leaving a clean-cut end.

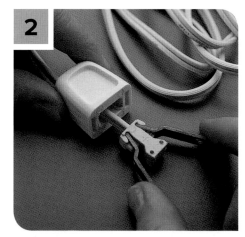

Feed unstripped wire through the rear of the plug casing. Spread the prongs, and then insert the wire into the opening in the rear of the core. Squeeze the prongs together; spikes inside the core penetrate the cord. Slide the casing over the core until it snaps into place.

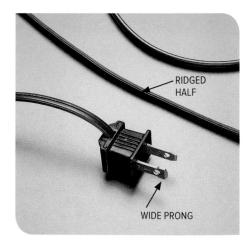

When replacing a polarized plug, make sure that the ridged half of the cord lines up with the wider (neutral) prong of the plug.

How to Replace a Round-Cord Plug

1 **Cut off the round cord** near the old plug using a combination tool. Remove the insulating faceplate on the new plug and feed the cord through the rear of the plug. Strip about 3" of outer insulation from the round cord. Strip ¾" insulation from the individual wires.

2 **Tie an underwriter's knot** with the black and the white wires. Make sure the knot is located close to the edge of the stripped outer insulation. Pull the cord so that the knot slides into the plug body.

UNDERWRITER'S KNOT

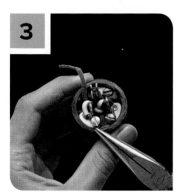

3 **Hook the end of the black wire** clockwise around the brass screw and the white wire around the silver screw. On a three-prong plug, attach the third wire to the grounding screw. If necessary, excess grounding wire can be cut away.

4 **Tighten the screws securely,** making sure the copper wires do not touch each other. Replace the insulating faceplate.

How to Replace a Flat-Cord Plug

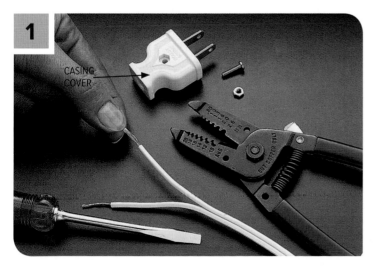

CASING COVER

Cut the old plug from cord using a combination tool. Pull apart the two halves of the flat cord so that about 2" of wire are separated. Strip ¾" insulation from each half. Remove the casing cover on the new plug.

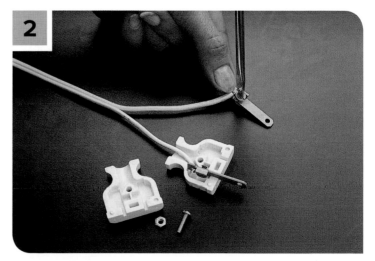

Hook the ends of the wires clockwise around the screw terminals and tighten the screw terminals securely. Reassemble the plug casing. Some plugs may have an insulating faceplate that must be installed.

How to Replace a Lamp Cord

1

With the lamp unplugged, the shade off, and the bulb out, you can remove the socket. Squeeze the outer shell of the socket just above the base and pull the shell out of the base. The shell is often marked "Press" at some point around its perimeter. Press there and then pull.

2

Under the outer shell, there is a cardboard insulating sleeve. Pull this off and you'll reveal the socket attached to the end of the cord.

3

With the shell and insulation set aside, pull the socket away from the lamp (it will still be connected to the cord). Unscrew the two screws to completely disconnect the socket from the cord. Set the socket aside with its shell (you'll need them to reassemble the lamp).

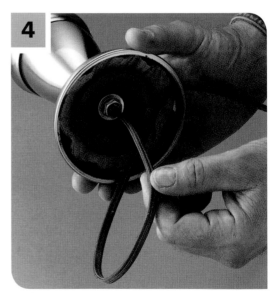

4

Remove the old cord from the lamp by grasping the cord near the base and pulling the cord through the lamp.

5

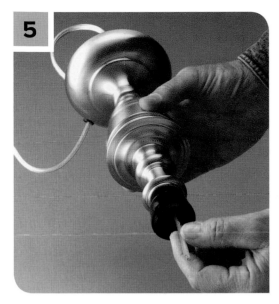

Bring your damaged cord to a hardware store or home center and purchase a similar cord set. (A cord set is simply a replacement cord with a plug already attached.) Snake the end of the cord up from the base of the lamp through the top so that about 3" of cord is visible above the top.

6

Carefully separate the two halves of the cord. If the halves won't pull apart, you can carefully make a cut in the middle with a knife. Strip away about ¾" of insulation from the end of each wire.

7

Connect the ends of the new cord to the two screws on the side of the socket (one of which will be silver in color, the other brass colored). One half of the cord will have ribbing or markings along its length; wrap that wire clockwise around the silver screw, and tighten the screw. The other half of the cord will be smooth; wrap it around the brass screw, and tighten the screw.

8

Set the socket on the base. Make sure the switch isn't blocked by the harp—the part that holds the shade on some lamps. Slide the cardboard insulating sleeve over the socket so the sleeve's notch aligns with the switch. Now slide the outer sleeve over the socket, aligning the notch with the switch. It should snap into the base securely. Screw in a lightbulb, plug the lamp in, and test it.

Making home plumbing repairs is easier than ever these days. The moving parts that are prone to failure tend to be located in cartridges or other systems that are designed to simply be removed and replaced. The trickiest part often is getting access, whether it be physically as when you are trying to reach up under a sink deck and loosen a nut; or loosening an old coupling that has corroded.

When it comes to drains, the two issues you are most likely to face are clogs and leaks. Freeing a clog is generally a mechanical process, although there are liquid or enzyme-based drain cleaners that claim to dissolve clogs. For immediate results, however, you'll need a plunger or a snake. Leaks in drain systems can be frustrated because they are most often caused by a loosened coupling or broken seal. Fixing them is usually a matter of remaking the bad connection or seal. This can get messy but is not especially difficult as long as you have access to the pipes or fittings. The good thing about a leaky drainline versus a leaky water supply lines is that, unlike supply lines, drains are not under pressure, so the effect of the leak is more likely a slow drip than a powerful, high-volume spray. There are bandage-type tricks you can do to slow or temporarily stop a leak in a supply line, but for a beginning home plumber this is a good time to call in a pro. The potential for major damage is too great to fiddle around and guess. But at the very least, learn where your water supply shutoff valves are so you can stop the water as soon as the leak is discovered.

Sinks, sink drains, faucets, and toilets are the fixtures that need repair attention most often. They are relatively simple to deal with in most cases: the trick is to locate the right replacement parts and do careful work that results in good, durable seals.

How to Shut Off the Water

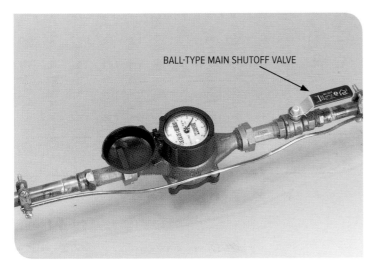

The main shutoff valve is located just inside your house at the point where the water supply enters—generally in the basement if you have one. Older shutoffs are "gate" types (above, right) that are turned clockwise to close. Newer ones (like the one above) tend to be ball valves with a handle that you turn to shut the valve. Shut off water at the main valve If you are unable to locate a shutoff at the branch line or at the fixture where the leak is occurring.

Branch-line shutoff valves control water supply to multiple fixtures in a specific area of your home. They generally appear in pairs, as the plumbing supply runs in parallel pipes (one hot, one cold). Gate valves are seen above. You can usually distinguish the hot line from the cold simply by feeling it. If you are unsure which is which, shut them both off in an emergency.

Fixture shutoff valves, often called stop valves, are located in an accessible spot next to an individual fixture such as a sink or toilet. Stop valves are required by code on new work, but many older fixtures may not have them, in which case locate the branch line shutoff valve or the main shutoff valve.

In-line supply tube shutoffs are located at points where a supply line has been tapped into to bring water to a low-demand fixture, such as an ice maker. Saddle valves like the one seen above are very common, but some codes do not allow them and professional plumbers seldom use them because they are prone to failure. Cutting the supply line and permanently installing a T-valve is a better (albeit more time-consuming) solution. On a saddle valve, you simply turn the handle to stop the water flow.

TOILET REPAIRS

A clogged toilet is one of the most common plumbing problems. If a toilet overflows or flushes sluggishly, clear the clog with a plunger or closet auger. If the problem persists, the clog may be in a branch drain or a drainage stack. Most other toilet problems are fixed easily with minor adjustments that require no disassembly or replacement parts. You can make these adjustments in a few minutes using simple tools. If minor adjustments do not fix the problem, further repairs will be needed. The parts of a standard toilet are not difficult to take apart, and most repair projects can be completed in less than 1 hour.

A recurring puddle of water on the floor around a toilet may be caused by a crack in the toilet base or in the tank. A damaged toilet should be replaced. Installing a new toilet is an easy project that can be finished in 3 or 4 hours.

An older toilet may have a tank ball that settles onto the flush valve to stop the flow of water into the bowl. The ball is attached to a lift wire, which is in turn attached to the lift rod. A ballcock valve is usually made of brass, with rubber washers that can wear out. If the ballcock valve malfunctions, you might be able to find old washers to repair it, but replacing both the ballcock and the tank ball with a float-cup assembly and flapper is easier and makes for a more durable repair.

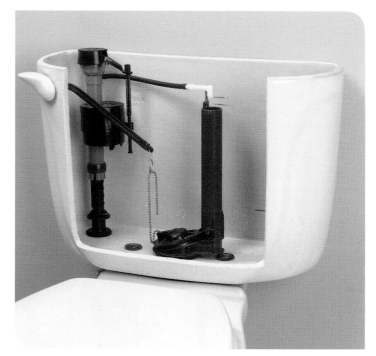

A modern float-cup valve with flapper is inexpensive and made of plastic, but it is more reliable than an old ballcock valve and ball.

Quick Fixes for Toilets

1

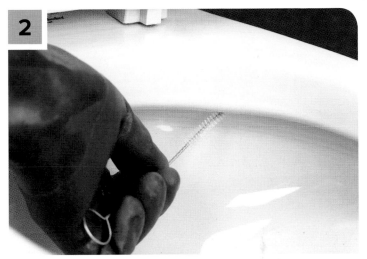

2

Phantom flushes? Phantom flushes are weak flushes that occur even when no one uses the handle. The flapper may not be completely sealing against the flush valve's seat. Make sure the chain is not tangled and that the flapper can go all the way down. If that does not solve the problem, shut off the water and drain the tank. If the problem persists, the flapper may need to be replaced.

Bowl not refilling well? The rim holes may be clogged. Most toilets have small holes on the underside of the bowl rim, through which water squirts during a flush. If you notice that some of these holes are clogged, use a stiff-bristled brush to clear out debris. You may need to first apply toilet bowl cleaner or mineral cleaner.

HOW TO ADJUST A TOILET HANDLE & LIFT

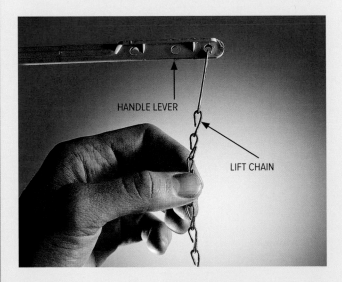

HANDLE LEVER

LIFT CHAIN

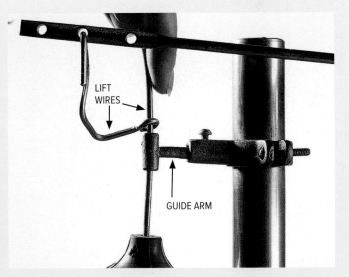

LIFT WIRES

GUIDE ARM

Lift chains. *Adjust the lift chain so it hangs straight from the handle lever, with about ½" of slack. Remove excess slack in the chain by hooking the chain in a different hole in the handle lever or by removing links with needle-nose pliers. A broken lift chain must be replaced.*

Lift wires. *Adjust the lift wires (found on older toilets without lift chains) so that the wires are straight and operate smoothly when the handle is pushed. A sticky handle often can be fixed by straightening bent lift wires. You can also buy replacement wires or replace the whole assembly with a float cup.*

Quick Fixes for Toilets

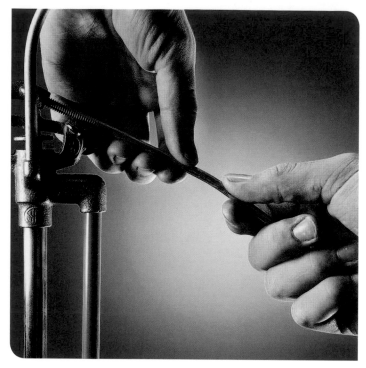

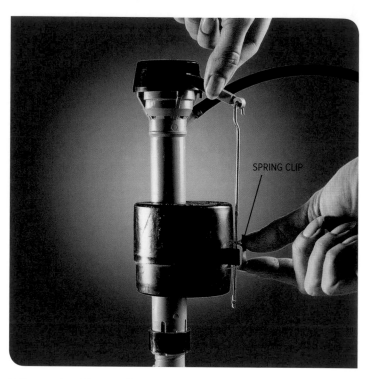

SPRING CLIP

Toilet running (ball float)? A ball float is connected to a float arm that's attached to a plunger on the other end. As the tank fills, the float rises and lifts one end of the float arm. At a certain point, the float arm depresses the plunger and stops the flow of water. By simply bending the float arm downward a bit, you can cause it to depress the plunger at a lower tank water level, solving the problem.

Toilet running (float cup)? A float-cup fill valve is made of plastic and is easy to adjust. Lower the water level by pinching the spring clip with fingers or pliers and moving the clip and cup down the pull rod and shank. Raise the water level by moving the clip and cup upward.

Toilet running (diaphragm fill valve)? A diaphragm-type fill valve usually is made of plastic and has a wide bonnet that contains a rubber diaphragm. Turn the adjustment screw clockwise to lower the water level and counterclockwise to raise it.

FLUSH INTERRUPTED? THREE WAYS FOR FIXING

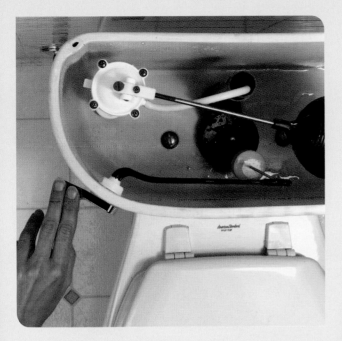

Sometimes there is plenty of water in the tank, but not enough of it makes it to the bowl before the flush valve shuts off the water from the tank. Modern toilets are designed to leave some water in the tank, since the first water that leaves the tank does so with the most force. To increase the duration of the flush, shorten the length of the chain between the flapper and the float (yellow in the model shown).

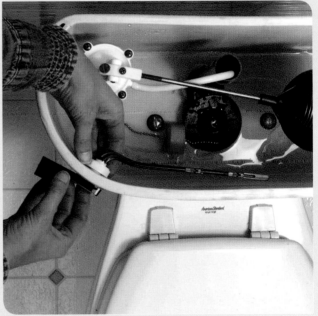

If the toilet is not completing flushes and the lever and chain for the flapper or tank ball are correctly adjusted, the problem could be that the handle mechanism needs cleaning or replacement. Remove the chain/linkage from the handle lever. Remove the nut on the backside of the handle with an adjustable wrench. It unthreads clockwise (the reverse of standard nuts). Remove the handle from the tank.

The handle lever should pull straight up on the flapper. If it doesn't, reposition the chain hook on the handle lever. When the flapper is covering the opening, there should be just a little slack in the chain. If there is too much slack, shorten the chain and cut off excess with the cutters on your pliers.

How to Replace a Toilet Fill Valve

Shut off the water supply at the fixture stop valve located on the tube that supplies water to the tank. Flush the toilet, and sponge out the remaining water. Loosen the coupling nut that attaches the supply tube to the toilet and disconnect the supply tube and mounting nut.

If the fill valve spins while you turn the mounting nut, hold the nut and the valve base with locking pliers. Lift out the old fill valve once it is disconnected.

Insert the properly adjusted fill valve into the tank opening, making sure the area around the tank opening is clean so the rubber washer seats properly.

From outside the tank, thread the locknut onto the threaded end of the valve shank. Hand tighten, then use a wrench to make an extra ¼ turn. Set the outlet end of the supply tube against the valve and then tighten the supply-tube coupling, first by hand then with a ¼ turn of a wrench. Do not overtighten.

5

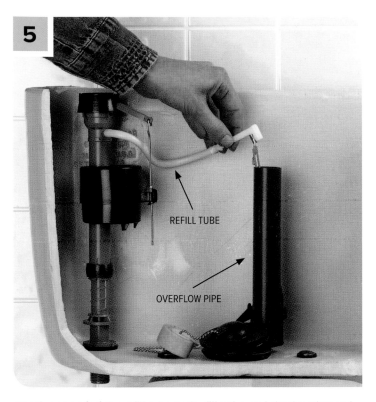

REFILL TUBE

OVERFLOW PIPE

Attach one end of the refill tube to the fill valve and clip the other end to the top of the overflow pipe (some overflow pipes have caps to which you connect the refill tube). The end of the tube should not project more than ¼" or so into the overflow pipe.

6

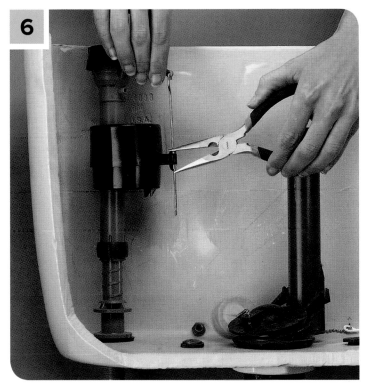

Turn the water on fully. Tighten any fitting that drips water. You can adjust the water level in the tank by squeezing the spring clip on the float cup with needle-nose pliers and moving the cup up or down on the link bar. Test the flush.

CRITICAL LEVEL LINES

The new fill valve and the overflow pipe each have a critical level ("CL") mark so you can set their relative heights in the toilet tank. The CL mark on the fill valve should be 1" above the CL line on the overflow pipe once the valve is installed. The height of the float cup on the fill valve can be adjusted up and down until the CLs are 1" apart. Place the fill valve in the opening at the tank bottom and check the CLs for alignment. Adjust the fill valve by rotating the telescoping mechanism (some types may have different adjustment mechanisms) and retesting until the valve CL is 1" above the pipe CL when seated in the tank opening.

How to Replace a Flush Valve

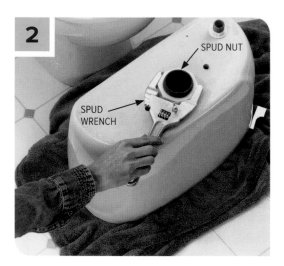

Unhook the chain from the handle lever arm and remove the tank. Carefully place it upside-down on an old towel. Remove the spud washer and spud nut from the base of the flush valve using a spud wrench or large channel-type pliers. Remove the old flush valve.

Replacing a flush valve requires that you remove the toilet tank from the stool. First disconnect the water supply tube from the fill valve (see step 1, previous page). Then unscrew the bolts holding the toilet tank to the bowl by loosening the nuts from below. If you are having difficulty unscrewing the tank bolts and nuts because they are fused together by rust or corrosion, apply penetrating oil or spray lubricant to the threads, give it a few minutes to penetrate, and then try again.

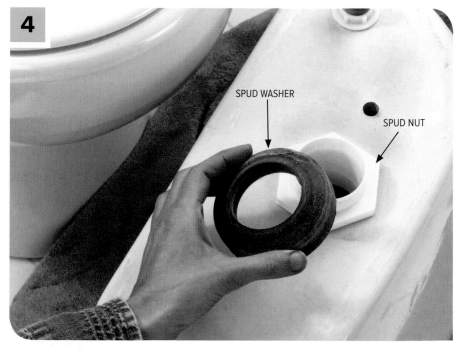

Place the new flush valve in the valve hole and check to see if the top of the overflow pipe is at least 1" below the critical level line (see previous page) and the tank opening where the handle is installed. If the pipe is too tall, cut it to length with a hacksaw.

Inside the tank, position the flush valve flapper and, from the tank underside, secure it with the spud nut. Tighten the nut ½ turn past hand tight with a spud wrench or large channel-type pliers. **CAUTION:** Overtightening may cause the tank to break. Place the spud washer over the spud nut.

5 INTERMEDIATE NUT GOES BETWEEN TANK AND BOWL

With the tank lying on its back, thread a rubber washer onto each tank bolt and insert the bolts into the bolt holes from inside the tank. Then, thread a brass washer and intermediate hex nut (an option that simply isolates the tank and bowl by creating a slight gap between them). Tighten to a quarter turn past hand tight.

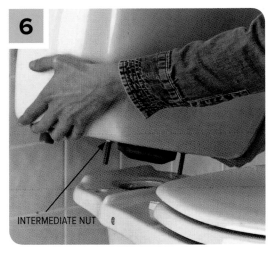

6 INTERMEDIATE NUT

With the hex nuts tightened against the tank bottom, carefully lower the tank over the bowl and set it down so the spud washer seats neatly over the water inlet in the bowl and the tank bolts fit through the holes in the bowl flange. Secure the tank to the bowl with a rubber washer, brass washer, and nut or wing nut at each bolt end. Press the tank to level as you hand-tighten the nuts. Hook up the water supply at the fill valve inlet.

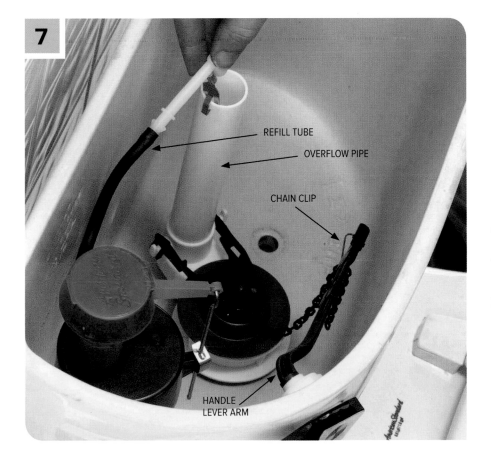

7 REFILL TUBE
OVERFLOW PIPE
CHAIN CLIP
HANDLE LEVER ARM

Connect the chain clip to the handle lever arm and adjust the number of links to allow for a little slack in the chain when the flapper is closed. Leave a little tail on the chain for adjusting, cutting off any excess. Attach the refill tube to the top of the overflow pipe. Turn on the water supply at the stop valve and test.

UNCLOGGING TOILETS

The toilet is clogged and has overflowed. Have patience. Now is the time for considered action. A second flush is a tempting but unnecessary gamble. First, do damage control. Mop up the water if there's been a spill. Next, consider the nature of the clog. Is it entirely "natural" or might a foreign object be contributing to the congestion? Push a natural blockage down the drain with a plunger. A foreign object should be removed, if possible, with a closet auger (sometimes called a snake). Pushing anything more durable than toilet paper into the sewer may create a more serious blockage in your drain and waste system.

If the tub, sink, and toilet all back up at once, the branch drainline that serves all the bathroom fixtures is probably blocked and your best recourse is to call a drain-clearing service.

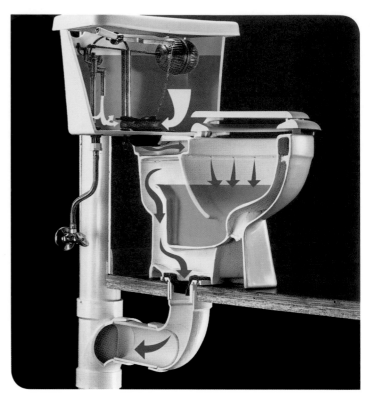

The trap is the most common catching spot for toilet clogs. Once the clog forms, flushing the toilet cannot generate enough water power to clear the trap, so flush water backs up. Traps on modern 1.6-gallon toilets have been redesigned to larger diameters and are less prone to clogs than the first generation of 1.6-gallon toilets.

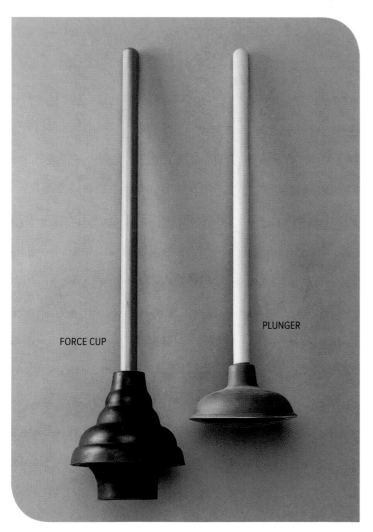

FORCE CUP

PLUNGER

Not all plungers are created equal. The standard plunger (left) is simply an inverted rubber cup and is used to plunge sinks, tubs, and showers. The flanged plunger, also called a force cup, is designed to get down into the trap of a toilet drain. You can fold the flange up into the flanged plunger cup and use it as a standard plunger.

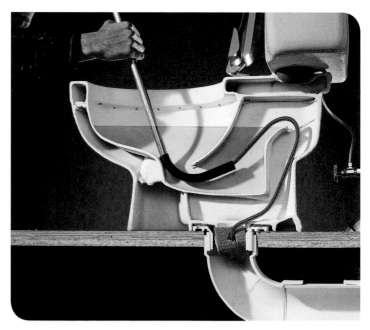

A closet auger is a semirigid cable housed in a tube. The tube has a bend at the end so it can be snaked through a toilet trap (without scratching it) to snag blockages.

How to Plunge a Clogged Toilet

Plunging is the easiest way to remove "natural" blockages. Take time to lay towels around the base of the toilet and remove other objects to a safe, dry location, since plunging may result in splashing. Often, allowing a very full toilet to sit for 20 or 30 minutes will permit some of the water to drain to a less precarious level.

There should be enough water in the bowl to completely cover the plunger. Fold out the skirt from inside the plunger to form a better seal with the opening at the base of the bowl. Pump the plunger vigorously six times, take a rest, and then repeat. Try this for four to five cycles.

TIP: If you force enough water out of the bowl that you are unable to create suction with the plunger, put a controlled amount of water in the bowl by lifting up on the flush valve in the tank. Resume plunging. When you think the drain is clear, you can try a controlled flush, with your hand ready to close the flush valve should the water threaten to spill out of the bowl.

How to Clear Clogs with a Closet Auger

PROTECTIVE RUBBER BOOT

Place the business end of the auger firmly in the bottom of the toilet bowl with the auger tip fully withdrawn. A rubber sleeve will protect the porcelain at the bottom bend of the auger. The tip will be facing back and up, which is the direction the toilet trap takes.

Rotate the handle on the auger housing clockwise as you push down on the rod, advancing the auger tip up into the trap. Work the cable back and forth as needed, but keep the rubber boot of the auger in the bowl. Rotate the auger counterclockwise to withdraw the blockage.

Fully retract the auger until you have recovered the object. This can be frustrating at times, but it is still a much easier task than the alternative—to remove the toilet and go fishing.

FIXING SINK FAUCETS

It's not surprising that sink faucets leak and drip. Any fitting that contains moving mechanical parts is susceptible to failure. But add to the equation the persistent force of water pressure working against the parts, and the real surprise is that faucets don't fail more often. It would be a bit unfair to say that the inner workings of a faucet are regarded as disposable by manufacturers, but it is safe to say that these parts have become easier to remove and replace.

The older your faucet, the more likely you can repair it by replacing small parts such as washers and O-rings. Many newer faucets can be repaired only by replacing the major inner components, such as a ceramic disk or a cartridge that encapsulates all the washers and O-rings that could possibly wear out.

The most important aspect of sink faucet repair is identifying which type of faucet you own. Here, we show all of the common types and provide instructions on repairing them. In every case, the easiest and most reliable repair method is to purchase a replacement kit with brand-new internal working parts for the model and brand of faucet you own.

Weak water flow? The first place to look is the aerator. Unscrew the aerator (essentially a filter) at the tip of the spout. If the filter screen is plugged, clean it carefully with an old toothbrush and some white vinegar. Rinse and replace the aerator.

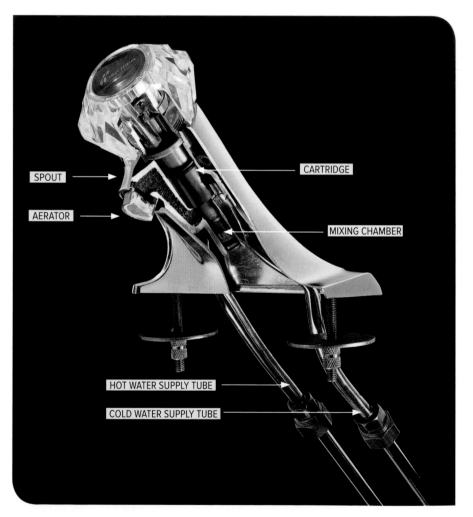

SPOUT

AERATOR

CARTRIDGE

MIXING CHAMBER

HOT WATER SUPPLY TUBE

COLD WATER SUPPLY TUBE

All faucets, no matter the type, have valves that move many thousands of times to open and close hot- and cold-water ports. These valves—or the rubber or plastic parts that rub against other parts when the faucet is being adjusted—wear out in time. Depending on the faucet, you may be able to fix the leak by cleaning or replacing small parts, such as washers or O-rings; or you may need to buy a repair kit and replace a number of parts; or the only solution may be to replace a self-enclosed cartridge that contains all the moving parts.

IDENTIFYING YOUR FAUCET TYPE AND REPLACEMENT PARTS

A leaky faucet is the most common home plumbing problem. Fortunately, repair parts are available for almost every type of faucet, from the oldest to the newest, and installing these parts is usually easy. But if you don't know your make and model, the hardest part of fixing a leak may be identifying your faucet and finding the right parts. Don't make the common mistake of thinking that any similar-looking parts will do the job; you've got to get exact replacements.

There are so many faucet types that even experts have trouble classifying them into neat categories. Two-handle faucets are either compression (stem) or washerless two-handle. Single-handle faucets are classified as mixing cartridge; ball; disc; or disc/cartridge. A single-handle faucet with a rounded, dome-shaped

cap is often a ball type. If a single-handle faucet has a flat top, it is likely a cartridge or a ceramic-disc type. An older two-handle faucet is likely of the compression type; newer two-handle models use washerless cartridges. Shut off the water, and test to verify that the water is off. Dismantle the faucet carefully. Look for a brand name: it may be clearly visible on the baseplate or printed on an inner part, or it may not be printed anywhere. Put all the parts into a reliable plastic bag and take them to your home center or plumbing supply store. A knowledgeable salesperson can help you identify the parts you need.

If you cannot find what you are looking for at a local store, check online faucet sites or the manufacturers' sites; they often have step-by-step instruction for identifying what you need. Note that manufacturers' terminology may not match the terms we use here. For example, the word "cartridge" may refer to a ceramic-disc unit.

To inspect the inner workings of your faucet, you first need to remove handles and spouts. You likely will need to pry off a cap on top of the handle or handles, but not always. The spout base housing is usually held in place with a small setscrew installed with an Allen wrench or small screwdriver.

Most faucets have corresponding repair kits, which include all the parts you need, and sometimes a small tool as well. Even if some of the parts in your faucet look fine, it's a good idea to install the parts provided by the kit to ensure against future wear. Kits usually are labeled by maker as well as by type.

How to Fix Compression Faucets

1

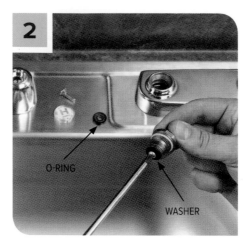

2

3

Pry off the cap on top of the handle and remove the screw that holds the faucet handle onto the stem. Pull the handle up and out. Use an adjustable wrench or pliers to unscrew the stem and pull it out.

Remove the screw that holds the rubber washer in place and pry out the washer. Replace a worn washer with an exact replacement—one that is the same diameter, thickness, and shape. Gently pry out the old O-ring and reinstall an exact replacement. Apply plumber's grease to the rubber parts before reinstalling the stem.

If washers wear out quickly, the seat is likely worn. Use a seat wrench to unscrew the seat from inside the faucet. Replace it with an exact duplicate. If replacing the washer and O-ring doesn't solve the problem, you may need to replace the entire stem.

COMPRESSION FAUCET

A compression faucet has a stem assembly that includes a retaining nut, threaded spindle, O-ring, stem washer, and stem screw. Dripping at the spout occurs when the washer becomes worn. Leaks around the handle are caused by a worn O-ring.

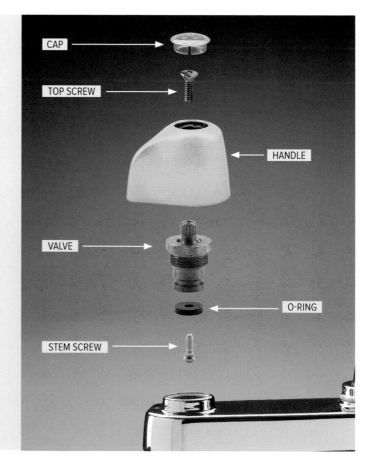

How to Fix Washerless Two-Handle Faucets

WASHERLESS TWO-HANDLE FAUCET

Almost all two-handle faucets made today are washerless. Instead of an older-type compression stem, there is a cartridge, usually with a plastic casing. Many of these cartridges contain ceramic discs, while others have metal or plastic pathways. No matter the type of cartridge, the repair is the same; instead of replacing small parts, you simply replace the entire cartridge.

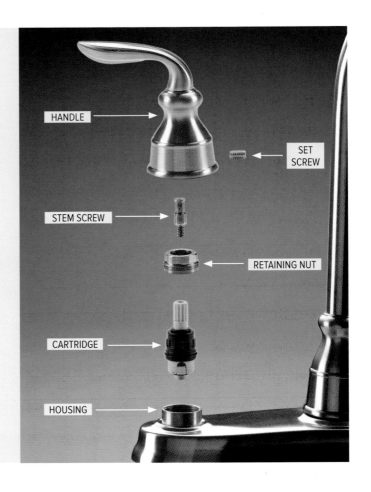

HANDLE

SET SCREW

STEM SCREW

RETAINING NUT

CARTRIDGE

HOUSING

1

RETAINING NUT

Remove the faucet handle and withdraw the old cartridge. Make a note of how the cartridge is oriented before you remove it. Purchase a replacement cartridge.

2

Install the replacement cartridge. Clean the valve seat first and coat the valve seat and O-rings with faucet grease. Be sure the new cartridge is in the correct position, with its tabs seated in the slotted body of the faucet. Reassemble the valve and handles and test.

How to Fix One-Handle Cartridge Faucets

To remove the spout, pry off the handle's cap and remove the screw below it. Pull the handle up and off. Use a crescent wrench to remove the pivot nut.

Lift out the spout. If the faucet has a diverter valve, remove it as well. Use a screwdriver or needle-nose pliers to pry out the retainer clip, which holds the cartridge in place.

ONE-HANDLE CARTRIDGE FAUCET

Single-handle cartridge faucets work by moving the cartridge up and down and side to side, which opens up pathways to direct varying amounts of hot and cold water to the spout. Moen, Price-Pfister, Delta, Peerless, Kohler, and others make many types of cartridges, some of which look very different from this one.

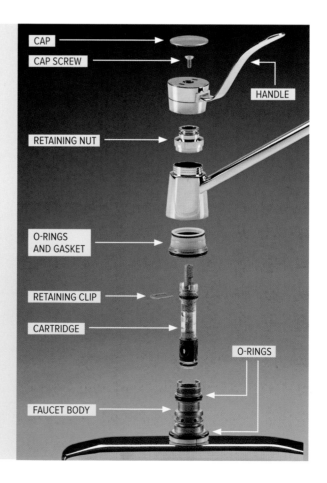

CAP

CAP SCREW

HANDLE

RETAINING NUT

O-RINGS AND GASKET

RETAINING CLIP

CARTRIDGE

O-RINGS

FAUCET BODY

3

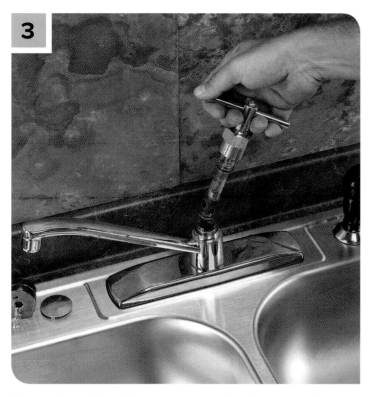

Remove the cartridge. If you simply pull up with pliers, you may leave part of the stem in the faucet body. If that happens, replace the cartridge and buy a stem puller made for your model.

4

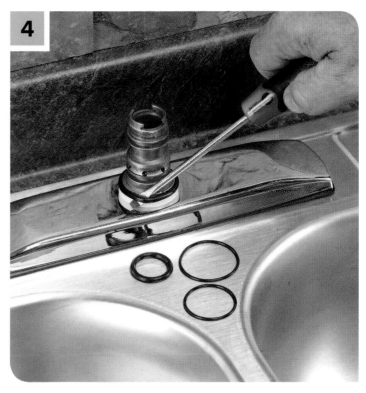

Gently pry out and replace all O-rings on the faucet body. Smear plumber's grease onto the new replacement cartridge and the new O-rings, reassemble the faucet, and test.

VARIATIONS: Here is one of many other types of single-handle cartridges. In this model, all the parts are plastic except for the stem, and it's important to note the direction in which the cartridge is aligned. If you test the faucet and the hot and cold are reversed, disassemble and realign the cartridge.

How to Fix Ball Faucets

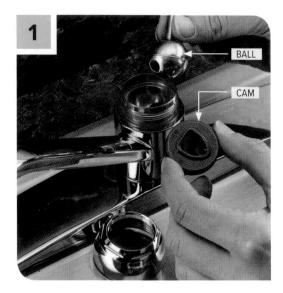

1

2

Remove the old ball and cam after removing the faucet handle and ball cap. Some faucets may require a ball faucet tool to remove the handle. Otherwise, simply use a pair of channel-type pliers to twist off the ball cap.

Pry out the neoprene valve seals and springs. Place thick towels around the faucet. Slowly turn on the water to flush out any debris in the faucet body. Replace the seals and springs with new parts. Also replace the O-rings on the valve body. You may want to replace the ball and cam too, especially if you're purchasing a repair kit. Coat all rubber parts in faucet grease, and reassemble the faucet.

BALL FAUCET

The ball-type faucet is used by Delta, Peerless, and a few others. The ball fits into the faucet body and is constructed with three holes (not visible here)—a hot inlet, a cold inlet, and the outlet, which fills the valve body with water that then flows to the spout or sprayer. Depending on the position of the ball, each inlet hole is open, closed, or somewhere in between. The inlet holes are sealed to the ball with valve seats, which are pressed tight against the ball with springs. If water drips from the spout, replace the seats and springs. Or go ahead and purchase an entire replacement kit and replace all or most of the working parts.

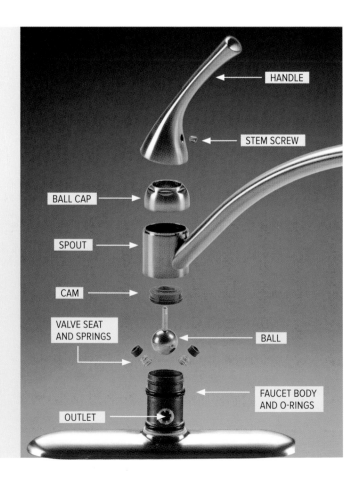

How to Fix Disc Faucets

DISC FAUCET

Disc-type faucets are the most common single-handle faucets currently being made. A pair of ceramic discs encased in a cylinder often referred to as a "cartridge" rub together as they rotate to open ports for hot and cold water. The ceramic discs do wear out in time, causing leaks, and there is only one solution—replace the disc unit/ cartridge. This makes for an easy—through comparatively expensive—repair.

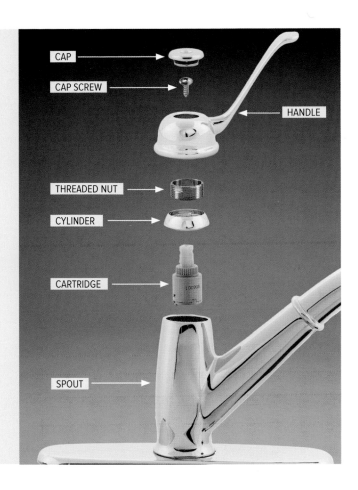

CAP

CAP SCREW

HANDLE

THREADED NUT

CYLINDER

CARTRIDGE

SPOUT

Replace the cylinder with a new one, coating the rubber parts with faucet grease before installing the new cylinder. Make sure the rubber seals fit correctly in the cylinder openings before you install the cylinder. Assemble the faucet handle.

KITCHEN SPRAYERS

If water pressure from a sink sprayer seems low, or if water leaks from the handle, it is usually because lime buildup and sediment have blocked small openings inside the sprayer head. To fix the problem, first take the sprayer head apart and clean the parts. If cleaning the sprayer head does not help, the problem may be caused by a faulty diverter valve. The diverter valve inside the faucet body shifts water flow from the faucet spout to the sprayer when the sprayer handle is pressed. Cleaning or replacing the diverter valve may fix water pressure problems.

Whenever making repairs to a sink sprayer, check the sprayer hose for kinks or cracks. A damaged hose should be replaced.

If water pressure from a faucet spout seems low, or if the flow is partially blocked, take the spout aerator apart and clean the parts. The aerator is a screw-on attachment with a small wire screen that mixes tiny air bubbles into the water flow. Make sure the wire screen is not clogged with sediment and lime buildup. If water pressure is low through out the house, it may be because galvanized steel water pipes are corroded. Corroded pipes should be replaced with copper pipes.

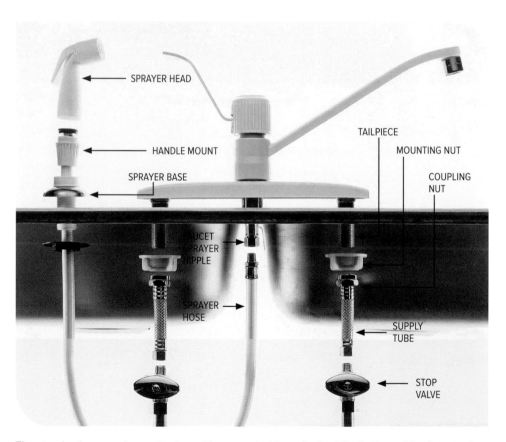

Replacing the diverter valve may solve low-flow problems if you do not wish to replace the entire sprayer. Diverter valves can usually be located by removing the faucet housing. Extract the valve, find a replacement, and reassemble the faucet and sprayer.

The standard sprayer hose attachment is connected to a nipple at the bottom of the faucet valve. When the lever of the sprayer is depressed, water flows from a diverter valve in the faucet body out to the sprayer. If your sprayer stream is weak or doesn't work at all, the chances are good that the problem lies in the diverter valve.

How to Replace a Sprayer Head

Replace a leaking sprayer head rather than the whole assembly to save money, time, and effort. Start by unscrewing the ridged base nut on the existing spray head. The spray head should come right off once the nut is entirely unscrewed.

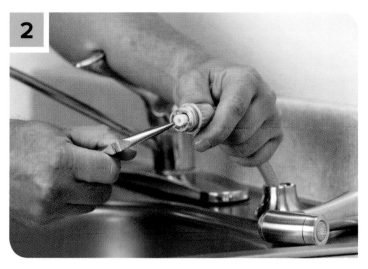

The spray head base is held in place by a small metal C-clip. Remove the rubber washer to expose the C-clip. Use needle-nose pliers to grab the clip and spread it until it pops out of its ridge and releases from the base. Remove the C-clip and base.

Secure the hose from slipping down the hole, if necessary. Buy a head to match the one you're replacing. Disassemble the new head and slide the new base onto the existing hose. Secure the base in place with a C-clip, cover with the rubber washer, and secure the sprayer on the base by hand-tightening the mounting nut.

SINK DRAINS

Every sink has a drain trap and a fixture drain line. Sink clogs usually are caused by a buildup of soap and hair in the trap or fixture drain line. Remove clogs by using a plunger, disconnecting and cleaning the trap, or using a hand auger. Many sinks hold water with a mechanical plug called a pop-up stopper. If the sink will not hold standing water, or if water in the sink drains too slowly, the pop-up stopper must be cleaned and adjusted.

Clogged lavatory sinks can be cleared with a plunger (not to be confused with a flanged force cup). Remove the pop-up drain plug and strainer first and plug the overflow hole by stuffing a wet rag into it, allowing you to create air pressure with the plunger.

How to Clear a Sink Trap

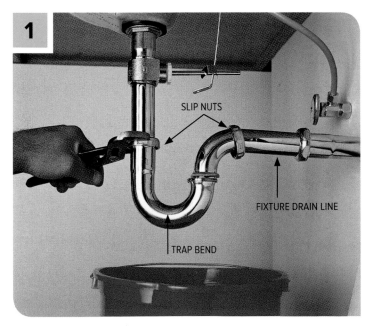

SLIP NUTS

FIXTURE DRAIN LINE

TRAP BEND

Place a bucket under the trap and loosen the slip nuts on the trap bend with channel pliers. Unscrew the nuts by hand and slip them away from the connections. Pull off the trap.

Remove any debris. Clean the trap bend with a small wire brush. Inspect the slip nut washers and replace if necessary. Reinstall the trap bend and tighten the slip nuts.

How to Clear a Kitchen Sink

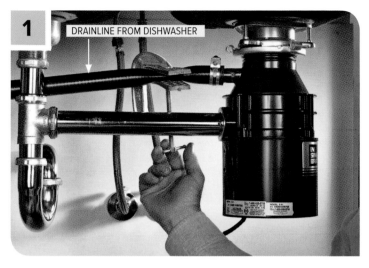

Plunging a kitchen sink is not difficult, but you need to create an uninterrupted pressure lock between the plunger and the clog. If you have a dishwasher, the drain tube needs to be clamped shut and sealed off at the disposal or drainline. The pads on the clamp should be large enough to flatten the tube across its full diameter (or you can clamp the tube ends between small boards).

If there is a second basin, have a helper hold a basket strainer plug in its drain or put a large pot or bucket full of water on top of it. Unfold the skirt within the plunger and place this in the drain of the sink you are plunging. There should be enough water in the sink to cover the plunger head. Plunge rhythmically for six repetitions with increasing vigor, pulling up hard on the last repetition. Repeat this sequence until the clog is removed. Flush out a cleared pipe with plenty of hot water.

How to Use a Hand Auger at the Trap Arm

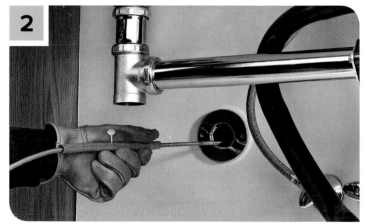

If plunging doesn't work, remove the trap and clean it out. With the trap off, see if water flows freely from both sinks (if you have two). Sometimes clogs will lodge in the tee fitting or one of the waste pipes feeding it. These may be pulled out manually or cleared with a bottlebrush or wire. When reassembling the trap, apply Teflon tape clockwise to the male threads of metal waste pieces. Tighten with your channel-type pliers. Plastic pieces need no tape and should be hand tightened only.

If you suspect the clog is downstream of the trap, remove the trap arm from the fitting at the wall. Look in the fixture drain with a flashlight. If you see water, that means the fixture drain is plugged. Clear it with a hand-crank or drill-powered auger.

FIXING TUB & SHOWER FAUCETS

Tub and shower faucets have the same basic designs as sink faucets, and the techniques for repairing leaks are the same as described in the faucet repair section of this book. To identify your faucet type, you may have to take off the handle and disassemble the faucet.

When a tub and shower are combined, the showerhead and the tub spout share the same hot and cold water supply lines and handles. Combination faucets are available as three-handle, two-handle, or single-handle types (see next page). The number of handles gives clues as to the design of the faucets and the kinds of repairs that may be necessary.

With combination faucets, a diverter valve or gate diverter is used to direct water flow to the tub spout or the showerhead. On three-handle faucet types, the middle handle controls a diverter valve. If water does not shift easily from tub to showerhead, or if water continues to run out the spout when the shower is on, the diverter valve probably needs to be cleaned and repaired.

Two-handle and single-handle types use a gate diverter that is operated by a pull lever or knob on the tub spout. Although gate diverters rarely need repair, the lever occasionally may break, come loose, or refuse to stay in the up position. To repair a gate diverter set in a tub spout, replace the entire spout.

Tub and shower faucets and diverter valves may be set inside wall cavities. Removing them may require a deep-set ratchet wrench. If spray from the showerhead is uneven, clean the spray holes. If the showerhead does not stay in an upright position, remove the head and replace the O-ring.

To add a shower to an existing tub, install a flexible shower adapter. Several manufacturers make complete conversion kits that allow a shower to be installed in less than one hour.

Tub/shower plumbing is notorious for developing drips from the tub spout and the showerhead. In most cases, the leak can be traced to the valves controlled by the faucet handles.

TUB & SHOWER COMBINATION FAUCETS

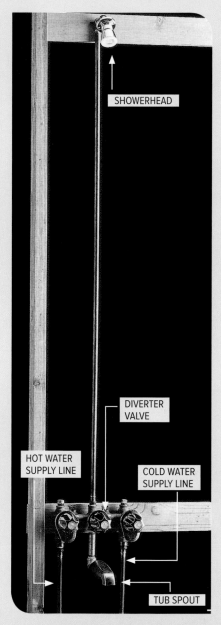

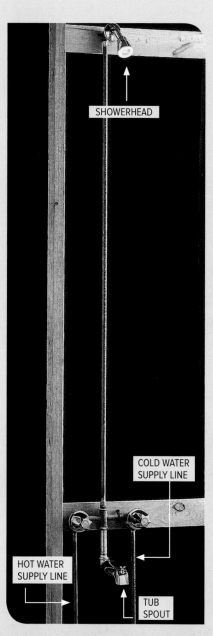

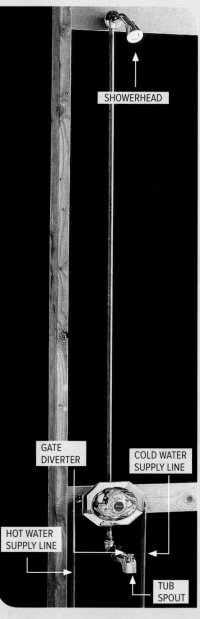

Three-handle faucets *have valves that are either compression or cartridge design.*

Two-handle faucets *have valves that are either compression or cartridge design.*

Single-handle faucets *have valves that are cartridge, ball-type, or disc design.*

Fixing Three-Handle Tub & Shower Faucets

A three-handle faucet type has two handles to control hot and cold water and a third handle to control the diverter valve and direct water to either a tub spout or a showerhead. The separate hot and cold handles indicate cartridge or compression faucet designs.

If a diverter valve sticks, if water flow is weak, or if water runs out of the tub spout when the flow is directed to the showerhead, the diverter needs to be repaired or replaced. Most diverter valves are similar to either compression or cartridge faucet valves. Compression-type diverters can be repaired, but cartridge types should be replaced. Remember to turn off the water before beginning work.

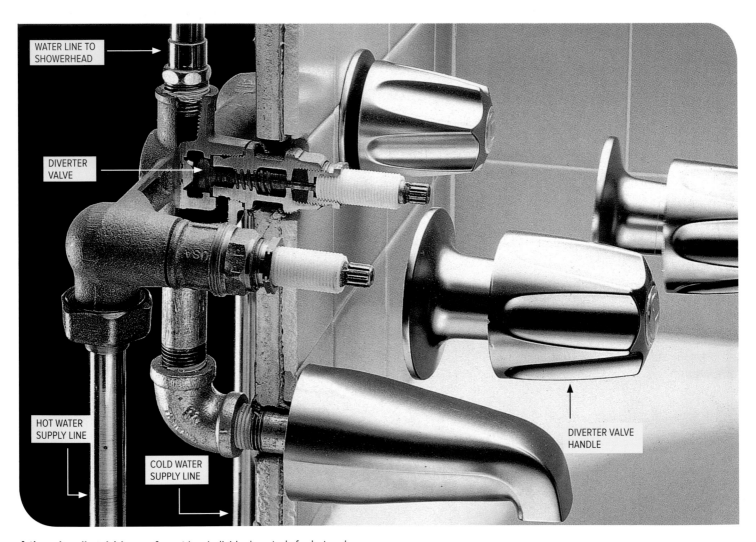

WATER LINE TO SHOWERHEAD

DIVERTER VALVE

HOT WATER SUPPLY LINE

COLD WATER SUPPLY LINE

DIVERTER VALVE HANDLE

A three-handle tub/shower faucet has individual controls for hot and cold water plus a third handle that operates the diverter valve.

How to Repair a Compression Diverter Valve

1

ESCUTCHEON

DIVERTER HANDLE

Remove the diverter valve handle with a screwdriver. Unscrew or pry off the escutcheon.

2

BONNET NUT

Remove the bonnet nut with an adjustable wrench or channel-type pliers.

3

Unscrew the stem assembly using a deep-set ratchet wrench. If necessary, chip away any mortar surrounding the bonnet nut.

4

STEM WASHER

STEM SCREW

Remove the brass stem screw. Replace the stem washer with an exact duplicate. If the stem screw is worn, replace it.

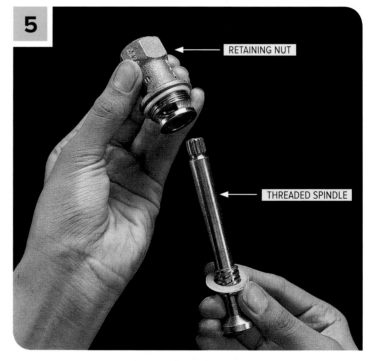

5

RETAINING NUT

THREADED SPINDLE

Unscrew the threaded spindle from the retaining nut. Clean sediment and lime buildup from the nut using a small wire brush dipped in vinegar. Coat all parts with faucet grease and reassemble the diverter valve.

Fixing Two-Handle Tub & Shower Faucets

Two-handle tub and shower faucets are either cartridge or compression design. Because the valves of two-handle tub and shower faucets may be set inside the wall cavity, a deep-set socket wrench may be required to remove the valve stem.

Two-handle tub and shower designs have a gate diverter, which is a simple mechanism located in the tub spout. A gate diverter closes the supply of water to the tub spout and redirects the flow to the showerhead. They seldom need repair. Occasionally, the lever may break, come loose, or refuse to stay in the up position.

If the gate diverter fails to work properly, replace the tub spout. Tub spouts are inexpensive and easy to replace.

Remember to turn off the water before beginning any work.

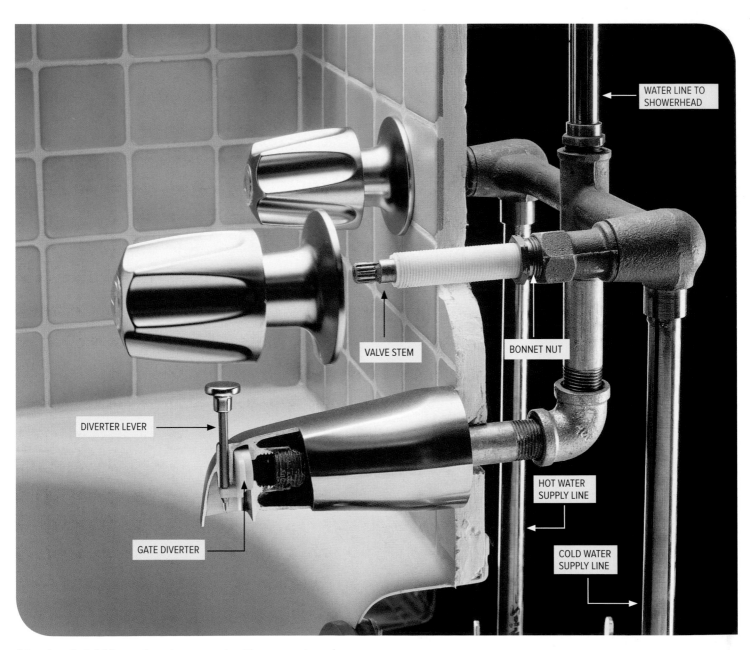

A two-handle tub/shower faucet can operate with compression valves, but more often these days they contain cartridges that can be replaced. Unlike a three-handle model, the diverter is a simple gate valve that is operated by a lever.

How to Remove a Deep-Set Faucet Valve

Remove the handle and unscrew the escutcheon with channel-type pliers. Pad the jaws of the pliers with masking tape to prevent scratching the escutcheon.

Chip away any mortar surrounding the bonnet nut using a ball-peen hammer and a small cold chisel.

Unscrew the bonnet nut with a deep-set ratchet wrench. Remove the bonnet nut and stem from the faucet body.

Fixing Single-Handle Tub & Shower Faucets

A single-handle tub and shower faucet has one valve that controls both water flow and temperature. Single-handle faucets may be ball, cartridge, or disc designs. If a single-handle control valve leaks or does not function properly, disassemble the faucet, clean the valve, and replace any worn parts. Repairing a single-handle cartridge faucet is shown on the opposite page.

Direction of the water flow to either the tub spout or the showerhead is controlled by a gate diverter. Gate diverters seldom need repair. Occasionally, the lever may break, come loose, or refuse to stay in the up position.

Remember to turn off the water before beginning any work; the shower faucet shown here has built-in shutoff valves, but many other valves do not. Open an access panel in an adjoining room or closet, behind the valve, and look for two shutoffs. If you can't find them there, you may have to shut off intermediate valves or the main shutoff valve.

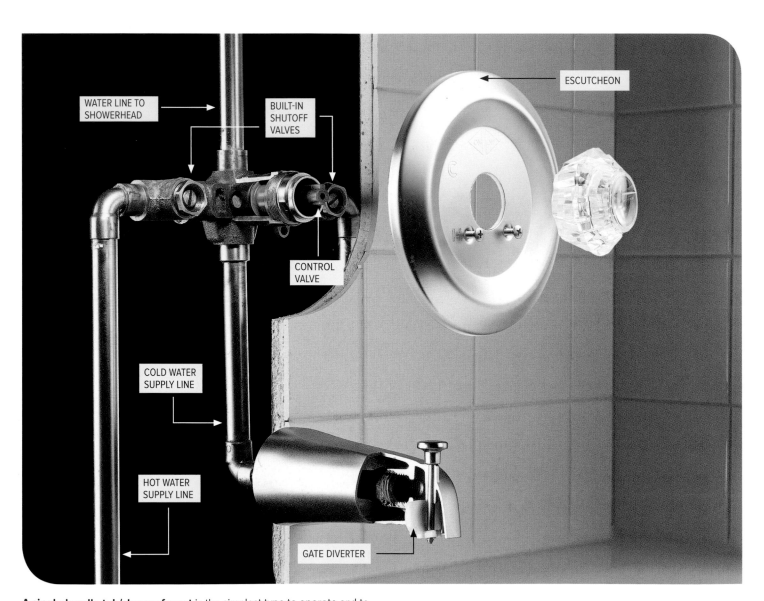

WATER LINE TO SHOWERHEAD

BUILT-IN SHUTOFF VALVES

ESCUTCHEON

CONTROL VALVE

COLD WATER SUPPLY LINE

HOT WATER SUPPLY LINE

GATE DIVERTER

A single-handle tub/shower faucet is the simplest type to operate and to maintain. The handle controls the mixing ratio of both hot and cold water, and the diverter is a simple gate valve.

How to Repair a Single-Handle Cartridge Tub & Shower Faucet

1

ESCUTCHEON

HANDLE

Use a screwdriver to remove the handle and escutcheon.

2

BUILT-IN SHUTOFF VALVES

Turn off the water supply at the built-in shutoff valves or the main shutoff valve.

3

BONNET NUT

Unscrew and remove the retaining ring or bonnet nut using adjustable-wrench.

4

O-RING

CARTRIDGE

Remove the cartridge assembly by grasping the end of the valve with channel-type pliers and pulling gently.

5

Flush the valve body with clean water to remove sediment. Replace any worn O-rings. Reinstall the cartridge and test the valve. If the faucet fails to work properly, replace the cartridge.

Single-Handle Tub & Shower Faucet with Scald Control

In many plumbing systems, if someone flushes a nearby toilet or turns on the cold water of a nearby faucet while someone else is taking a shower, the shower water temperature can suddenly rise precipitously. This is not only uncomfortable; it can actually scald you. For that reason, many one-handle shower valves have a device, called a "balancing valve" or an "antiscald valve," that keeps the water from getting too hot.

The temperature of your shower may drastically rise to dangerous, scalding levels if a nearby toilet is flushed. A shower fixture equipped with an antiscald valve prevents this sometimes dangerous situation.

How to Adjust the Shower's Temperature

To reduce or raise the maximum temperature, remove the handle and escutcheon. Some models have an adjustment screw, others have a handle that can be turned by hand.

To remove a balancing valve, you may need to buy a removal tool made for your faucet. Before replacing, slowly turn on water to flush out any debris; use a towel or bucket to keep water from entering the inside of the wall.

FIXING & REPLACING SHOWERHEADS

I f spray from the showerhead is uneven, clean the spray holes. The outlet or inlet holes of the showerhead may get clogged with mineral deposits. Showerheads pivot into different positions. If a showerhead does not stay in position, or if it leaks, replace the O-ring that seals against the swivel ball.

A tub can be equipped with a shower by installing a flexible shower adapter kit. Complete kits are available at hardware stores and home centers.

A typical showerhead can be disassembled easily for cleaning and repair. Some showerheads include a spray adjustment cam lever that is used to change the force of the spray.

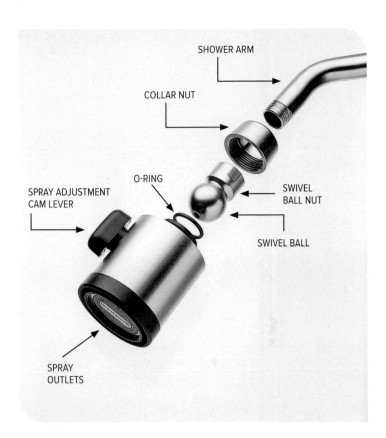

How to Clean & Repair a Showerhead

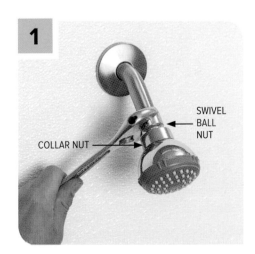

Unscrew the swivel ball nut using an adjustable wrench or channel-type pliers. Wrap the jaws of the tool with masking tape to prevent marring the finish. Unscrew the collar nut from the showerhead.

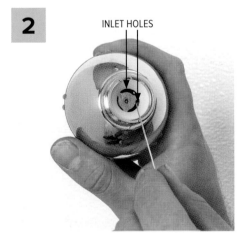

Clean outlet and inlet holes of the showerhead with a thin wire. Flush the head with clean water.

Replace the O-ring, if necessary. Lubricate the O-ring with faucet grease before installing.

How to Replace a Showerhead with a Handheld Spray Head

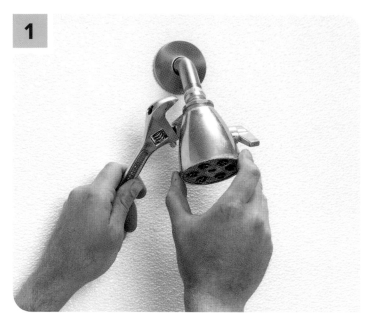

1

Make sure when shopping for a new handheld showerhead that the head mounting bracket is compatible with your existing shower arm. Ask an associate for help if you're not sure. Remove the existing fixed head by unscrewing the mounting nut with channel-lock pliers.

2

Attach the new showerhead mounting bracket by screwing the mounting nut end onto the end of the shower arm (you don't need Teflon tape for this because the bracket has an internal rubber washer). Hand-tighten the bracket until it is snug and the large side of the mounting slot on the end is pointing up and the hose connection is pointing down.

3

Attach the mounting nut end of the showerhead hose to the hose connection on the bracket. Hand-tighten the hose mounting nut. Do not use pliers for this.

4

Screw the showerhead base onto the conical end of the showerhead hose and slip the cone base into the mounting bracket. Turn on the water and check that there are no leaks. If you find any, turn the water off and hand-tighten the connection further until it does not leak.

NOTE: The hose may curl up awkwardly; time and exposure to hot water will soon slacken the hose to hang normally.

CREDITS & RESOURCES

FLOORS

Aacer Flooring
Solid and engineered hardwood
www.aacerflooring.com

Elmwood Reclaimed Timber
Plank and endgrain floors, stairs,
wood vents
www.elmwoodreclaimedtimber.com

Forest Stewardship Council
www.us.fsc.org

Hardwood Floors Magazine of the
National Wood Flooring Association
www.hardwoodfloorsmag.com

Shaw Floors
Solid and engineered hardwood,
laminate
www.shawfloors.com

Teragren
Bamboo
www.teragren.com

Urban Floor
Solid and engineered hardwood
www.urbanfloor.com

WALLS & CEILINGS

3M
Masking Paper and 3M
888-364-3577
www.3m.com

Fypon Ltd.
800-446-3040
www.fypon.com

The Steel Network, Inc.
888-474-4876
www.steelnetwork.com

WINDOWS & DOORS

Access One, Inc
800-561-2223
www.lifewaymobility.com

Andersen Windows, Inc.
800-426-4261
www.andersenwindows.com

The Bilco Company
203-934-6363
www.bilco.com

Designer Doors
800-241-0525
www.cambek.com

JELD-WEN, Inc.
800-877-9482
www.jeld-wen.com

Kolbe Windows & Doors
715-842-56666
www.kolbewindows.com

Kwikset Corporation
1-800-327-5625
www.kwikset.com

Larson Manufacturing
888-483-3768
www.larsondoors.com

Madawaska Doors, Inc.
800-263-2358
www.madawaska-doors.com

Marvin Windows and Doors
888-537-7828
www.marvin.com

Milgard Windows
800-MILGARD (1-800-645-4273)
www.milgard.com

Roto Frank of America
800-787-7709
800-243-0893
roto-frank.com/us

Simpson Door Company
800-952-4057
www.simpsondoor.com

VELUX America, Inc.
800-888-3589
www.velux-america.com

Wheatbelt, Inc.
800-264-5171
www.rollupshutter.com

WIRING & LIGHTING

Pass & Seymour Legrand
Home automation products
877 295 3472
www.passandseymour.com

Westinghouse
Ceiling fans, decorative lighting,
solar outdoor lighting, & other
lighting fixtures and bulbs
866 442 7873
Purchase here:
www.budgetlighting.com
www.westinghouse.com

PLUMBING

American Standard
Bathroom fixtures including
toilets, tubs, sinks, and suites
www.americanstandard.com
(800) 442-1902

Bestbath
ADA and ANSI-compliant universal
design fixtures and accessories
www.bestbath.com
(800) 727-9907

Duravit
Bathroom, sinks, and bathroom
furniture
www.duravit.us

Interstyle
Ceramic and glass tiles
interstyleglass.com
(800) 667-1566

Moen
Faucets, shower and bath fixtures,
lighting, accessories, and
bathroom safety accessories
www.moen.com

MTI
Tubs, shower bases and enclo-
sures, sinks, and accessories
mtibaths.com
(800) 783-8827

National Kitchen and Bath
Association (NKBA)
Industry association offering
advice and listings of professionals
by area
www.nkba.org
(800) 843-6522

POWER TOOLS & ACCESSORIES

Black & Decker
800-544-6986
www.blackanddecker.com

METRIC CONVERSIONS

Metric Conversions

TO CONVERT:	TO:	MULTIPLY BY:
Inches	Millimeters	25.4
Inches	Centimeters	25.4
Feet	Meters	0.305
Yards	Meters	0.914
Square inches	Square centimeters	6.45
Square feet	Square meters	0.093
Square yards	Square meters	0.836
Ounces	Milliliters	30.0
Pints (U.S.)	Liters	0.473 (Imp. 0.568)
Quarts (U.S.)	Liters	0.946 (Imp. 1.136)
Gallons (U.S.)	Liters	3.785 (Imp. 4.546)
Ounces	Grams	28.4
Pounds	Kilograms	0.454

TO CONVERT:	TO:	MULTIPLY BY:
Millimeters	Inches	0.039
Centimeters	Inches	0.394
Meters	Feet	3.28
Meters	Yards	1.09
Square centimeters	Square inches	0.155
Square meters	Square feet	10.8
Square meters	Square yards	1.2
Milliliters	Ounces	.033
Liters	Pints (U.S.)	2.114 (Imp. 1.76)
Liters	Quarts (U.S.)	1.057 (Imp. 0.88)
Liters	Gallons (U.S.)	0.264 (Imp. 0.22)
Grams	Ounces	0.035
Kilograms	Pounds	2.2

Converting Temperatures

Convert degrees Fahrenheit (F) to degrees Celsius (C) by following this simple formula: Subtract 32 from the Fahrenheit temperature reading. Then, multiply that number by $\frac{5}{9}$. For example, 77°F - 32 = 45. 45 × $\frac{5}{9}$ = 25°C.

To convert degrees Celsius to degrees Fahrenheit, multiply the Celsius temperature reading by $\frac{9}{5}$. Then, add 32. For example, 25°C × $\frac{9}{5}$ = 45. 45 + 32 = 77°F.

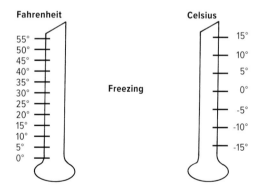

Metric Plywood Panels

Metric plywood panels are commonly available in two sizes: 1,200 mm × 2,400 mm and 1,220 mm × 2,400 mm, which is roughly equivalent to a 4 × 8-ft. sheet. Standard and Select sheathing panels come in standard thicknesses, while Sanded grade panels are available in special thicknesses.

STANDARD SHEATHING GRADE		SANDED GRADE	
7.5 mm	($\frac{5}{16}$ in.)	6 mm	($\frac{4}{17}$ in.)
9.5 mm	($\frac{3}{8}$ in.)	8 mm	($\frac{5}{16}$ in.)
12.5 mm	($\frac{1}{2}$ in.)	11 mm	($\frac{7}{16}$ in.)
15.5 mm	($\frac{5}{8}$ in.)	14 mm	($\frac{9}{16}$ in.)
18.5 mm	($\frac{3}{4}$ in.)	17 mm	($\frac{2}{3}$ in.)
20.5 mm	($\frac{13}{16}$ in.)	19 mm	($\frac{3}{4}$ in.)
22.5 mm	($\frac{7}{8}$ in.)	21 mm	($\frac{13}{16}$ in.)
25.5 mm	(1 in.)	24 mm	($\frac{15}{16}$ in.)

Lumber Dimensions

NOMINAL - U.S.	ACTUAL - U.S. (IN INCHES)	METRIC
1 × 2	¾ × 1½	19 × 38 mm
1 × 3	¾ × 2½	19 × 64 mm
1 × 4	¾ × 3½	19 × 89 mm
1 × 5	¾ × 4½	19 × 114 mm
1 × 6	¾ × 5½	19 × 140 mm
1 × 7	¾ × 6¼	19 × 159 mm
1 × 8	¾ × 7¼	19 × 184 mm
1 × 10	¾ × 9¼	19 × 235 mm
1 × 12	¾ × 11¼	19 × 286 mm
1¼ × 4	1 × 3½	25 × 89 mm
1¼ × 6	1 × 5½	25 × 140 mm
1¼ × 8	1 × 7¼	25 × 184 mm
1¼ × 10	1 × 9¼	25 × 235 mm
1¼ × 12	1 × 11¼	25 × 286 mm
1½ × 4	1¼ × 3½	32 × 89 mm
1½ × 6	1¼ × 5½	32 × 140 mm
1½ × 8	1¼ × 7¼	32 × 184 mm
1½ × 10	1¼ × 9¼	32 × 235 mm
1½ × 12	1¼ × 11¼	32 × 286 mm
2 × 4	1½ × 3½	38 × 89 mm
2 × 6	1½ × 5½	38 × 140 mm
2 × 8	1½ × 7¼	38 × 184 mm
2 × 10	1½ × 9¼	38 × 235 mm
2 × 12	1½ × 11¼	38 × 286 mm
3 × 6	2½ × 5½	64 × 140 mm
4 × 4	3½ × 3½	89 × 89 mm
4 × 6	3½ × 5½	89 × 140 mm

Liquid Measurement Equivalents

1 Pint	= 16 Fluid Ounces	= 2 Cups
1 Quart	= 32 Fluid Ounces	= 2 Pints
1 Gallon	= 128 Fluid Ounces	= 4 Quarts

Drill Bit Guide

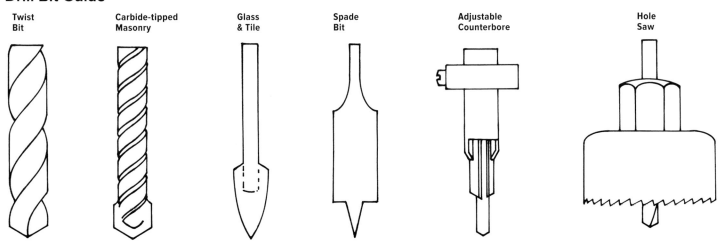

Twist Bit	Carbide-tipped Masonry	Glass & Tile	Spade Bit	Adjustable Counterbore	Hole Saw

Nails

Nail lengths are identified by numbers from 4 to 60 followed by the letter "d," which stands for "penny." For general framing and repair work, use common or box nails. Common nails are best suited to framing work where strength is important. Box nails are smaller in diameter than common nails, which makes them easier to drive and less likely to split wood. Use box nails for light work and thin materials. Most common and box nails have a cement or vinyl coating that improves their holding power.

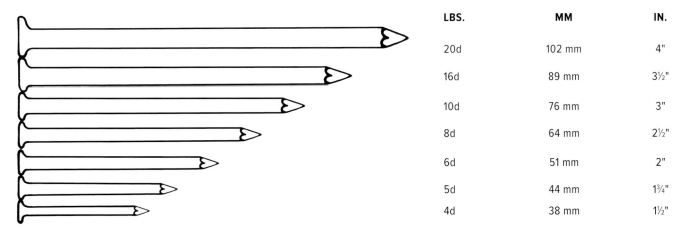

LBS.	MM	IN.
20d	102 mm	4"
16d	89 mm	3½"
10d	76 mm	3"
8d	64 mm	2½"
6d	51 mm	2"
5d	44 mm	1¾"
4d	38 mm	1½"

Counterbore, Shank & Pilot Hole Diameters

SCREW SIZE	COUNTERBORE DIAMETER FOR SCREW HEAD (IN INCHES)	CLEARANCE HOLE FOR SCREW SHANK (IN INCHES)	PILOT HOLE DIAMETER	
			HARD WOOD (IN INCHES)	SOFT WOOD (IN INCHES)
#1	.146 (⁹⁄₆₄)	⁵⁄₆₄	³⁄₆₄	¹⁄₃₂
#2	¼	³⁄₃₂	³⁄₆₄	¹⁄₃₂
#3	¼	⁷⁄₆₄	¹⁄₁₆	³⁄₆₄
#4	¼	⅛	¹⁄₁₆	³⁄₆₄
#5	¼	⅛	⁵⁄₆₄	¹⁄₁₆
#6	⁵⁄₁₆	⁹⁄₆₄	³⁄₃₂	⁵⁄₆₄
#7	⁵⁄₁₆	⁵⁄₃₂	³⁄₃₂	⁵⁄₆₄
#8	⅜	¹¹⁄₆₄	⅛	³⁄₃₂
#9	⅜	¹¹⁄₆₄	⅛	³⁄₃₂
#10	⅜	³⁄₁₆	⅛	⁷⁄₆₄
#11	½	³⁄₁₆	⁵⁄₃₂	⁹⁄₆₄
#12	½	⁷⁄₃₂	⁹⁄₆₄	⅛

INDEX